SOUTHERN INDUSTRY
AND
REGIONAL DEVELOPMENT

SOUTHERN INDUSTRY AND REGIONAL DEVELOPMENT

By

HARRIET L. HERRING

RESEARCH ASSOCIATE, INSTITUTE FOR RESEARCH IN SOCIAL SCIENCE,
UNIVERSITY OF NORTH CAROLINA

With a Foreword by

HOWARD W. ODUM

DIRECTOR, INSTITUTE FOR RESEARCH IN SOCIAL SCIENCE,
UNIVERSITY OF NORTH CAROLINA

CHAPEL HILL
THE UNIVERSITY OF NORTH CAROLINA PRESS
1940

COPYRIGHT, 1941, BY

THE UNIVERSITY OF NORTH CAROLINA PRESS

PREFACE

The role of industry in regional development has always been a fundamental one. It has a distinguished heritage in America, both in theory and in the practical economy of the nation. Perhaps the most common illustration that comes to the mind of the average observer is the case of New England and the later Northeast and still later Middle Western industrial-metropolitan concentration of wealth and industries. In the southern United States there may be found one of the best examples in the rise of textile manufacturing in the cotton South. The vividness of this example has been emphasized in the continuing debate on the effect of moving cotton manufacturing out of New England to the South, and more recently in the national discussions of the need for a more balanced economy as between agriculture and industry in the Southern States.

It has been said that the South is the best documented region of the United States. For a long time much of this writing was done by the other regions. But the South has for some time been busy examining itself. More recently it has been equally busy seeking the methods and the means for doing something about itself. Especially is this true in regard to industrial development. For despite theories of the inexorableness of economic laws of business enterprise and industrial location, the South firmly believes that by taking thought it can add a cubit to its stature. It did this in the instance already cited; by conscious will and effort the region built its chief industry. It is trying now to correct the unbalance both within itself and relative to the rest of the country. Many Southerners think that the next few years are particularly important because of the demands and opportunities of the national defense program and collateral developments.

For such examination and such efforts there is need for general principles and for factual data that will be helpful in concrete situations. This study proposes one such unifying principle which may be useful to planners: an application to manufacturing industry of Professor Howard W. Odum's principle of optimum production. It supplies some simple—it is hoped not oversimplified—indices that may be useful to agencies trying to encourage manufacturing.

As suggested above, I am indebted to Dr. Odum first for the idea and later for the encouragement to make of its application something more than a few rough notes on a set of interesting figures. I am also indebted to a number of my colleagues in the University and the Institute for assistance and for helpful criticisms, especially to Mrs. Nadia Danilevsky for concentrated aid with the statistics, to Mrs. Treva Williams Bevacqua and Miss Anne Tillinghast for expert and patient work in preparation of the manuscript, and to Professor Rupert B. Vance for editing it.

H. L. H.

Chapel Hill
October 30, 1940

FOREWORD

The people of the South and of the Nation are concerned with few themes more than with the role of industry in regional development. Indeed there are few people and perhaps no institutions that are not vitally concerned with such balanced economy as will enable the region to develop and utilize wisely its resources, give employment to its abundance of workers, contribute to the development, education, and welfare of its people, and enrich the culture and well-being of the Nation.

Miss Herring's volume on *Southern Industry and Regional Development* appears peculiarly appropriate at this time. It is not only timely in the total framework of industry and national defense and in the relation of industrial location to national policy, but is especially important in the total framework of permanent defense and prosperity. With reference to the southern regions, it is a distinctive unit in the general framework of "The South at Its Best," interpreted as attainable standards of economy and culture, a theme to which the Institute for Research in Social Science at the University of North Carolina has for many years devoted a major portion of its purposive research. It is, moreover, an important unit in the larger framework of regional-national planning in the new and dynamic sense, in which the nation is seeking its new strength and integration through the development and strengthening of its diverse regions. Furthermore, the book presents a vivid challenge to all those who hold that the South constitutes the most important testing ground for American regionalism and a working manual for those who are ready to achieve.

It is important to emphasize not only the importance of this program of optimum development, but also something of its meaning. As Miss Herring points out, *optimum* means the best that can be done in the total framework of the South itself, of the other regions, of the total national and international balance, and in relation to geographic, cultural, population, and time factors. We re-emphasize, therefore, two characteristics: the one in relation to the nation and the other in relation to the southern regions, and in this volume, the Southeastern States as presented in *Southern Regions of the United States*. This first emphasis is that the southern regions of the United States are a component part of a great nation, whose development and well-being depend upon the corresponding development and well-being of all regions integrated and correlated to the best possible degree. The nation has now come to recognize that one way to make the American dream come true is to make it possible for the people in each of the regions of our country to achieve the ends desired. We have come to see that the way to make a strong nation is to create strong regions; the way to make strong regions is to balance people with resources; the way to redistribute wealth is to create the capacity to produce and to use wisely in each region; the way to develop children and youth is to give them opportunity in their own regional setting; and always the balance of men and resources to be achieved through the democratic process.

The second point of emphasis on the nature of the program is that "The South at Its Best" implies no specific panacea, no single-type program, no exclusive values, but always has its assumptions well bottomed in the growth of the region through the work of its people, the development of its resources, and through the cooperative processes of community and government. It must be clear, therefore, that our statement of desirable and attainable ends of southern regional development must be in terms that are flexible, comprehensive, enduring, and commensurate with the cultural, economic, and social framework of our American democracy. Our attainable standards must be stated in terms of capacities of growth, of development of natural resources and people, of the devotion of the people and their wealth to institutional services through which we seek a balance and equilibrium between the people and wealth, between men and technology, between culture and civilization. We do not, therefore, say "The South at Its Best" is a wealthy South, or an industrial South, or an agrarian South; but we say that "The South at Its Best" is a growing South, a developing South, utilizing, developing, and conserving all of its resources in a balanced economy, of, for, and by the people, and of, for, and by all of the institutions. Its specific objectives and its specific needs will then be worked out in relation to each diversified phase of life, each changing situation, and in the combined and cooperative work of all acting together. Our statement, therefore, of what the South needs to be at its best is not something very specific in the field of education or industry or labor or capital, but it is the development of all of its people and capacities.

By indicating the relation of industry, as presented in this study, to the total southern regional development, we may point up perhaps in an oversimplified way the strategic importance of this subject. We may recall that in an inventory of the southern regions, it has been estimated that the South excels in two of the basic sources of wealth that go into the making of an enduring economy and lags in three. That is, it has a superabundance of natural resources and of human resources, but lags in the skill, training, and technology necessary to translate its resources into capital wealth. It is, therefore, poor and lags in the support of many of its institutions. The assumption is that if it could train its people, develop skills, science, and education, through which it would then develop and conserve its resources, it would immediately excel in all five of the types of wealth, namely, natural wealth, technological wealth, capital wealth, human wealth, and institutional wealth.

It must be clear that the goals to be sought focus clearly upon the wise use of the two sources of wealth in which we excel, namely, natural wealth and human wealth. In so far as the South is not utilizing its resources through planning, conservation, and new reaches in manufacturing, industry, and agriculture, it cannot give employment to its superabundance of people, without which in turn it is not possible for the region to share that common American heritage of prosperity and welfare.

We may indicate further the role of industry in this program by recalling some of the immediate elementary tasks that await the South if it is to seek these attainable standards of culture and economy which will vouchsafe the South its leading part in the new American scene.

First is the problem of educating the new generation of the South to sense the meaning of natural wealth and its relation to the living realities of the people and their welfare; this includes a sensing of the value of work and high standards of achievement. Second is the problem of widening the range of occupational opportunity, through new developments, to the end that the superabundance of southern youth may have a chance to work, and thus to develop and use our resources. The third task is, then, actually to train and equip these youth so that they may function adequately and in competition with workers everywhere.

Manifestly, more capital wealth is necessary for the undertaking of these tasks. This wealth must come from several sources: from the South's own economic gains in line with the extraordinary progress that has been made in the last few years; from the investment of wealth owned by southerners who are joining in the new frontiers of southern development; from investments of those who live outside the region, but who see in it an opportunity for regional and national development; from national foundations whose monies in research and experimentation can give leverage to regional support; and from the Federal Government in equalization program—agriculture, roads, health, education, public safety, and the like.

It is evident that our youth at the present time do not have a sense of the real meaning of natural wealth, of standards of work, of achievement. It has not been fashionable either for boys or girls to be interested in soil erosion, natural resources, conservation, waste of men, and waste of soil, or in social problems. One of the most pathetic spectacles of our whole situation is that of the most attractive youth in the world literally hanging around drugstores and way places, wondering what it is all about and what to do next.

With reference to the widening range of occupational opportunity, it must be clear now that scarcely more than half of our southern youth can hope to have equal opportunity in the old sense of the American dream —opportunity to work, to create, to have families, and to find security. There must be new avenues through increasing industry and the balance between industry and agriculture and increased opportunity for trained leaders.

It must be clear also with reference to the third need that at the present time our southern youth are not trained to do anything very well. In an age of scarcity and need for work, for engineering, for skills, for farming, for dairying, it is not possible to find personnel equipped to do the jobs that must be done and in reality jobs that the youth themselves would want to do if they knew about them and were so equipped.

It must be clear, therefore, why these tasks are part and parcel of the whole southern program—the schools, the universities, the towns, the cities, rural communities, the national and local governments, the national and local civic organizations and chambers of commerce. It must be clear that this is literally a program of, for, and by all the people and all the institutions, and that there is no one throughout the broad reaches of the region who should not have a portion in the development of this part of the American dream of opportunity. Thus, it is no longer tenable to say that the development of industry belongs to this or that group or is limited to this or that function of economy.

Immediately, it is argued, of course, that this task is a difficult task. It is. There are problems of interregional relations and problems of conflict in economic interest. There are problems of labor and problems of capital to be readjusted. There are problems of untrained people and the cumulative handicaps of a region. But by and large these are standard problems and are all involved in the attainment of the objectives which have been suggested. Thus, our academic queries become matters of very practical concern when we ask:

How many and what sort of new and old industries
Will give occupation to how many people
Who in turn will create purchasing power
To enable how many more people to remain on the farm
To produce commodities of what sort
In turn to provide raw materials for what other industries
Which in turn will employ how many more workers
Who in turn will become skilled

FOREWORD

Who in turn will continue the cycle
Seeking to approximate the better balanced region
Of attainable standards of culture and economy?

Now in the past most discussions of this problem have been very general; most efforts fortuitous or at least scarcely well planned. In contrast, here is a volume giving many facts about the 352 types of manufacturing in the Nation; more specific facts about those that are more related to the South and its potentialities; all set in the framework of indices which can be utilized in southern regional development. This has not been done before; it has long been needed. Here is in reality the making of an actual working manual which should be in the hands of all students and statesmen and of all industrialists, planning groups, councils of governors, chambers of commerce, boards of trade and all that great host of others who seek the ends of the best possible southern regional development.

It is a far cry from the abstract discussions of the agrarians, of the industrialists, the professors, and the idealists to this challenge to test and try out these formulae, for, as Miss Herring points out, "The solution will not just grow. It will take something more positive to create in the South a healthy balance within itself and allow it to make its greatest contribution to the national well-being." But "with a broad philosophy that is fundamentally sound it should be possible to work toward details that will be equally sound, even down to specific industries for specific states."

So, too, it is pointed out that there is a negative side, namely, that "along with planning for optimum production must go firm, if gradual, planning to correct production of a kind that is unsound and unhealthy."

Finally, here are two types of challenging statements that ought to be tested. One is that such an examination of the situation as is presented in this book "will reveal the directions in which the Southeast has pushed its industrial development far enough, and the directions in which it could wisely plan for, and encourage expansion." And another is that "the reasons for the lack of skills in the Southeast boil down to lack of manufacturing in which to learn and practice skills."

In the service of the desired southern regional development and of an inquiring South and Nation, this study and others to follow will be offered with the hope that they can and will be used effectively and immediately. The next volume to appear, namely, Milton S. Heath's "The Structure of Southern Industry," will undoubtedly prove to be one of the most valuable contributions yet made.

Howard W. Odum.

CONTENTS

	PAGE
PREFACE	V
FOREWORD BY HOWARD W. ODUM	vii

Chapter I
AN OPTIMUM MANUFACTURING ECONOMY FOR THE SOUTHEAST 3

Chapter II
MANUFACTURING FOR THE NATION—GROUP I INDUSTRIES 10

Chapter III
MANUFACTURING FOR THE REGION—GROUP II INDUSTRIES 36

Chapter IV
MANUFACTURING FOR REGIONAL BALANCE—GROUP III INDUSTRIES 54

Chapter V
OPTIMUM PRODUCTION AND OPPORTUNITY 70

Chapter VI
THE STATISTICAL PICTURE 81

INDEX 97

SOUTHERN INDUSTRY
AND
REGIONAL DEVELOPMENT

CHAPTER I

AN OPTIMUM MANUFACTURING ECONOMY FOR THE SOUTHEAST

Industry, particularly manufacturing industry, is needed in the South. It is needed to enrich the region and the nation. It is needed to balance production and consumption, and to achieve a better balance between agriculture and manufacturing. To this end every state is trying to entice manufacturing to its borders, trying to stimulate its citizens to build and operate manufacturing establishments. Councils of governors, industrial councils, and sometimes official agencies of the states, sponsor programs designed to do both these things and to remove handicaps in the way of industrial development for the whole South.

Most of these activities are on either a fortuitous or an opportunistic basis. Advertisements announce the advantages of climate, labor, favorable attitudes of the public and other tangible and intangible resources, in a blind effort to attract a new entrepreneur or an old one dissatisfied with his present location. Any suggestion of interest by inquiry or by rumor is followed by supplying data, by high-pressure salesmanship, by offers of inducements on the part of towns or cities. The same methods are undoubtedly employed to attract some industries without any preliminary indication of interest on their part, on the general knowledge that certain types of manufacturing are hard pressed in their present locations.

There are three fundamental defects in this method of securing industries for the South or a state in the South. In the first place, it is obviously more apt than not to attract weak industries which pay low wages and make small profits. The South has specialized in that type of industry long enough. It is unnecessary to produce here a mass of statistics to prove this point. Later in the discussion figures for other purposes will abundantly illustrate this sort of concentration in the South.

In the second place, this method is apt to attract more of the same sorts of industry which a state or the region already has. Industries, the same or related, are gregarious. They find some quite concrete advantages in going to a place already inhabited by their kind: capital, materials, supplies, and markets or established channels for securing all these, as well as a trained labor force. They find some intangibles that are no less important: the give and take among neighboring managers—there is nobody so lonely as the manager of a plant in a state far from all his fellows; the sheer weight of an important industry in local, state, and regional affairs—city councils, state legislatures, and regional blocs in Congress keep an eye and ear attuned to its needs, problems, and advantages.

But the South, out of its painful experience with two- or three-crop commercial agriculture and two- or three-industry manufacturing, needs no more, but rather less, concentration in a few lines. Casual observation and the most elementary statistics show that the wealthiest and most stable states are those that have the most varied economic base.

In the third place, this method of developing industry is too hit-or-miss, too dependent on the whim or judgment of some manager, or upon the sales ability of a representative of some chamber of commerce. It has no relation to the fundamental resources of a state or region per se or as a part of the nation, nor to its needs viewed over a long period of time. It has no conscious relation to the national economy. Unconsciously or accidentally it often runs counter to a sound national policy. It is completely planless.

Hit-or-miss development, artificial stimulus, selfishness or preoccupation in other regions, and carelessness in the South have contributed to the economic problems of this region. The solution will not just grow. It will take something more positive to create in the South a healthy balance within itself and allow it to make its greatest contribution to the national wellbeing.

Americans have talked of social and economic planning for some time. For the most part this talk has been in a desultory or an academic fashion, or in a defensive or apologetic manner. Under the pressure of recent events the interest is becoming more practical. The depression taught us that the nation is not economically or socially healthy if any large sector of it is ill, whether it be a geographical region, an economic class, a racial group or even a few important industries. The war in Europe is teaching us that the United States is facing a future which no longer permits the assumption that because we have great natural resources and an energetic, aggressive people, we shall always have plenty; that we can always expand production and markets; that we can be prodigal of our wealth or wasteful in our methods; or that we can assume security and abundance in an undesigned workaday world.

In the search for realistic planning there has been much experiment and exploration. Beginning first with the cities and metropolitan regions, the planning movement has grown until it encompasses well-nigh the whole of our society. The nation, the states, cities and counties, and even special localities have set up groups or boards to formulate plans for various types of development. In the South such boards, still unevenly distributed and hesitating, are replacing or paralleling the older agencies for enticing manufactures. They are acutely interested in industrial development and in a better balance between agriculture and manufacturing.

Much of the work of such boards, like that of chambers of commerce, so far has been directed primarily toward taking thought for today, namely toward getting a pay roll for a town full of unemployed people. It must be very clear now that this is not enough; they must take thought for tomorrow as well, and not only for the town but for the state and the nation. Without a broad philosophy that is economically and socially sound this hothouse growth may be futile. Nay, more than futile: it may harm the soil from which it is uprooted and require permanent artificial nurture where it is transplanted. With a broad philosophy that is fundamentally sound it should be possible to work toward details that will be equally sound, even down to specific industries for specific states.

The key to such a philosophy may be found in the premises of planning for optimum production as set forth in *Southern Regions of the United States*.[1] And optimum production really means the best: for the long run, for the well-being of regions and nation, for the utilization of resources and skills, for economy of production and distribution. To be sure such a principle cannot be formulated, much less applied, in a vacuum. It must take into account the differences which now exist. And so, along with planning for optimum production must go firm, if gradual, planning to correct production of a kind that is unsound and unhealthy.

For a nation like the United States with its varied resources and peoples and its great free-trade market, the principle of optimum production as applied to manufactures resolves itself into three subprinciples:

I. A state or a region should manufacture for the national market those goods for which it is peculiarly suited because of climate, of natural and agricultural resources, and of skills. In this way each would contribute most to the national economy.

II. In addition, a state or region should manufacture for its own use goods for the production of which it has sufficient resources and skills. In this way each would give its own industrial development the balance which comes from variety, and would lessen the social and economic waste of advertising, selling and transporting goods crisscross over a continent.

III. Finally, a state or region should develop, at least for its own use, the manufacture of those goods for which it could economically and profitably produce the raw materials and develop its potential skills. In this way

[1] Howard W. Odum, *Southern Regions of the United States*. See specifically pp. 447, 449.

it would add further variety and balance to its manufactures, help to balance its agricultural economy, and provide more varied opportunities for its people.

With these principles as a guide an examination of the present situation will show in what ways the Southeast measures up in this sort of program at present, in what ways it is deficient. It will show why development which accidentally or partially fulfills one or even two of these principles may still be less than good, to say nothing of optimum, production. It is believed that such an examination will reveal the directions in which the Southeast has pushed its industrial development far enough, and the directions in which it could wisely plan for, and encourage expansion.

The most complete exposition of the present status in manufacturing industries of the United States is the *Biennial Census of Manufactures*. For, while it covers only a few items, it attempts to cover at least these for all manufacturing. And so its statistics on wage earners, wages, salaried persons, salaries, value of product and value added by manufacture have been used to construct what is, for lack of a better name, a set of very simple indices in order that the states, the region, and specific industries can be compared.

The best unit of comparison is the wage earner. There are many reasons for this. In the first place it is the basis most easily understood. When we speak of a large plant we usually have in mind the fact that it employs many workers. The iron and steel group and the textile group are considered the greatest industries in the country because they employ the most workers; New York is ranked the greatest industrial state because it has the most wage earners. In the second place, interest in industry in the Southeast, and in the United States for the last decade as well, has been pointed toward its potentialities as an employer. Thirdly, it is better than any other available base. In some respects capital might be as good, though it would emphasize an interest in dollars rather than in people. But the facts about capital are quite literally unknown for any single industry, to say nothing of all industries. The use of wages as a base puts a premium on the low wage industry, making its other factors look unduly favorable because the wage is so small. Finally, the wage earner base is already in common use by such agencies as the Bureau of Labor Statistics and the National Industrial Conference Board for a wide variety of statistics on manufacturing.

And so, though it is itself imperfect because of the wide variation in the application of labor to machinery, the wage earner base is better than most. It emphasizes the interest of the region and the nation in employment, it is available, and it is a perfectly understandable and commonly used unit. The number of wage earners given in the census for a state or an industry

OPTIMUM MANUFACTURING

is an average of the number employed on the fifteenth of each month, so that seasonal fluctuations are minimized. For various technical reasons,[2] the chief one being that there is no distinction between full-time and part-time workers, the number averages somewhat larger than the full-time wage earners. Therefore all "per wage earner" figures tend to be slightly smaller than a true average, and in this study are always referred to as "wage, (etc.) per wage earner" rather than as "average wage," etc. And in any case, the chief purpose here is a comparison of industries. Throughout this study the census of 1937 is used except for comparison with earlier years when these are helpful, though such comparisons leave something to be desired because of changes in the value of the dollar, the increase in mechanization, and the ups and downs of the depression. Other sources are used sparingly because of the difficulty of getting comparable classifications.

In order to give a general picture this index has been applied first of all to the data for the states and regions. This supplies standards of comparison for the Southeast and for the specific industries. The number of wage earners is shown in the accompanying and all other tables in order to make vivid the importance of the state or the industry discussed.

By way of preview we may anticipate some striking facts which emerge from this comparison. The eleven states of the Southeast have 14.2 percent of the wage earners in manufacturing industries of the United States. But they have considerably less of the manufacturing industries by other measures: 9.1 percent of the wages, 10.5 percent of the value of product, 9.6 percent of the value added by manufacture, 8.0 percent of the salaried persons and 7.2 percent of the salaries. The wage per wage earner for all industries in the United States is $1,180; for the Southeast it is $759. In only three states outside the Southeast, Maine, New Hampshire, and New Mexico, does this figure fall below $1,000; in not a single southeastern state does it reach $1,000.

"Value added by manufacture" is an equally important factor. This is the balance after cost of raw materials, fuel, power, supplies, etc. is deducted from value of product. Out of it must come wages, salaries, taxes, capital costs such as interest and amortization, profit, and sundry minor costs. The average value added by manufacture per wage earner for all industry in the United States is $2,938. Not a state in the Southeast reaches that amount. In only four states in the Southeast does this figure reach $2,000; in only one state outside the Southeast, New Hampshire, does it fall below $2,000. For industry to be profitable for the whole community the value added by manufacture must be high, not only in order for wages and salaries to be high, but also to meet capital costs and taxes. This is particu-

[2] See *Biennial Census of Manufactures, 1937*, Part I, pp. 7-8.

larly true of high capital cost industries or of a state if it specializes in industries which require a large amount of capital investment per wage earner. Satisfactory data on capital investment in the several states are not available, but it seems unlikely that New York, for example, would have nearly two and one-half times as much capital invested per wage earner as South Carolina. New York has nearly 300,000 wage earners (some 30 percent of its total) in clothing industries which require little capital—probably considerably less than $1,000 per wage earner. South Carolina has some 88,000 of its total 129,000 wage earners in cotton mills which require around $3,000 capital investment per wage earner. In New York the value added by manufacture per wage earner is $3,331, in South Carolina $1,352. Similar comparisons could be made between other states, for example, Alabama and Kansas.

The Southeast is deficient in skills, particularly on the technical level. It has either developed industries which do not require many technical persons, or else gets along with few of this type of workers. A rough measure of this fact is in the number of salaried persons per wage earner. The bare mechanics of work supervision, of record keeping, and of clerical and office operation require a certain minimum number of salaried workers in any industry; very marked differences in so large a composite as all the industries of a state or region are partly explained by the difference in number of the more skilled supervisors, laboratory workers, engineers, etc. Further verification of this will be discussed in Chapter V. Suffice it here to point out that there are 12.5 wage earners to each salaried worker in the Southeast compared with only 7 in the whole United States and somewhat less in the great industrial regions of the Northeast and Middle States. In the amount expended for salaries per wage earner the same is true: in the Southeast the figure is $162; in every other region it is twice that amount. This is not explained by lower salaries in the Southeast. The region and its several states compare rather favorably with the rest of the country on this score. It is mainly accounted for by the smaller number of salaried persons.

The accompanying table of the states and regions shows these and many other points. It gives national, regional and state averages for comparison with each other and with any given industry. In addition it indicates the pattern of succeeding tables and illustrates the application of the "per wage earner" index to data for the several states as it will be applied to that for the various industries.

OPTIMUM MANUFACTURING

Indices of Manufacturing Industries, 1937
States, Regions, and the United States

State and Region	Total wage earners	Wages per wage earner	Value of product per wage earner	Value added by mfr. per wage earner	Percent wages are of value added by mfr.	Salary per salaried person	Salary per wage earner	Number of wage earners per salaried person	Wage and salary per wage earner	Percent wages and salary are of value added by mfr.	Balance per wage earner for interest, profits, taxes, etc.
UNITED STATES..	8,569,231	$ 1,180	$ 7,085	$ 2,938	40.2	$ 2,232	$ 317	7.0	$ 1,497	51.0	$ 1,441
SOUTHEAST........	1,216,412	759	5,221	1,987	38.2	2,030	162	12.5	921	46.4	1,066
Virginia.............	132,643	850	6,847	2,532	33.6	2,153	191	11.3	1,041	41.1	1,491
North Carolina.......	258,771	731	5,351	1,839	39.7	2,211	112	19.7	843	45.8	996
South Carolina.......	129,748	707	3,159	1,352	52.3	2,179	91	23.9	798	59.0	554
Georgia.............	159,496	693	4,443	1,690	41.0	1,883	148	12.7	841	49.8	849
Florida.............	52,005	702	4,174	1,998	35.1	1,740	231	7.6	933	46.7	1,065
Kentucky...........	68,998	960	7,318	2,636	36.4	2,079	265	7.8	1,225	46.5	1,411
Tennessee..........	135,073	809	5,242	2,189	37.0	2,039	202	10.2	1,011	46.2	1,178
Alabama...........	120,301	798	4,769	1,974	40.4	2,096	154	13.6	952	48.2	1,022
Mississippi.........	46,040	573	4,141	1,656	34.6	1,780	124	14.4	697	42.1	959
Arkansas...........	37,280	663	4,417	1,759	37.7	1,875	163	16.5	826	47.0	933
Louisiana..........	76,057	792	7,637	2,628	30.1	1,962	249	7.9	1,041	39.6	1,587
SOUTHWEST........	169,928	1,050	12,279	3,491	30.1	1,939	347	5.6	1,397	40.0	2,094
Oklahoma..........	29,551	1,164	12,388	3,743	31.1	1,997	408	4.9	1,572	42.0	2,171
Texas..............	129,501	1,023	12,212	3,397	30.1	1,919	334	5.7	1,357	39.9	2,040
New Mexico........	3,683	812	5,593	2,475	32.8	1,518	209	7.2	1,021	41.3	1,454
Arizona............	7,193	1,196	16,454	4,676	25.6	2,192	392	5.6	1,588	34.0	3,088
NORTHEAST........	3,668,255	1,190	6,402	2,886	41.2	2,299	341	6.7	1,531	53.0	1,355
Maine..............	75,464	958	4,620	2,002	47.9	2,091	178	11.7	1,136	56.7	866
New Hampshire.....	56,517	977	4,417	1,864	52.4	2,173	185	11.7	1,162	62.3	702
Vermont............	23,682	1,039	4,724	2,242	46.3	2,103	255	8.2	1,294	57.7	948
Massachusetts......	496,036	1,121	5,283	2,533	44.3	2,259	311	7.3	1,432	56.5	1,101
Rhode Island.......	108,031	1,045	4,787	2,226	46.9	2,331	267	8.7	1,312	58.9	914
Connecticut........	262,620	1,189	4,805	2,592	45.9	2,213	312	7.1	1,501	57.9	1,091
New York..........	995,658	1,241	7,346	3,331	37.3	2,327	441	5.2	1,682	50.5	1,649
New Jersey.........	436,745	1,199	7,449	3,120	38.4	2,378	368	6.5	1,567	50.2	1,553
Pennsylvania.......	954,340	1,233	6,321	2,792	44.2	2,308	297	7.8	1,530	54.8	1,262
Delaware...........	21,052	1,092	5,908	2,774	39.4	2,362	301	7.9	1,393	50.2	1,381
Maryland...........	145,932	1,076	7,509	2,952	36.4	2,212	279	7.9	1,355	45.9	1,597
District of Columbia...	8,714	1,474	8,504	4,895	30.1	1,888	1,093	1.7	2,567	52.4	2,328
West Virginia.......	83,464	1,228	5,757	2,669	46.0	2,270	219	10.3	1,447	54.2	1,222
MIDDLE STATES.....	2,915,765	1,335	7,930	3,277	40.7	2,267	343	6.6	1,678	51.2	1,599
Ohio................	694,205	1,379	7,346	3,323	41.5	2,335	350	6.7	1,729	52.0	1,594
Indiana.............	313,342	1,283	7,971	3,252	39.5	2,145	298	7.2	1,581	48.6	1,671
Illinois..............	668,841	1,290	7,931	3,467	37.2	2,316	409	5.6	1,699	49.0	1,768
Michigan...........	660,676	1,494	8,016	3,166	47.2	2,406	278	8.7	1,772	56.0	1,394
Wisconsin..........	234,067	1,266	7,572	3,033	41.7	2,137	352	6.1	1,618	53.3	1,415
Minnesota..........	89,925	1,194	10,425	3,480	34.3	2,062	399	5.2	1,593	45.8	1,887
Iowa...............	67,878	1,123	10,452	3,478	32.3	1,836	376	4.9	1,499	43.1	1,979
Missouri............	186,831	1,084	8,057	2,999	36.1	2,145	343	6.3	1,427	47.6	1,572
NORTHWEST........	128,428	1,205	13,306	3,547	34.0	1,889	399	4.7	1,604	45.2	1,943
North Dakota.......	2,854	1,119	16,061	3,597	31.1	1,708	502	3.4	1,621	45.1	1,976
South Dakota.......	4,970	1,104	13,536	2,893	38.2	1,716	442	3.9	1,546	53.4	1,347
Nebraska...........	19,590	1,129	14,421	3,442	32.8	1,847	462	4.0	1,591	46.2	1,851
Kansas.............	34,128	1,187	15,934	3,731	31.8	1,859	457	4.1	1,644	44.1	2,087
Montana...........	11,268	1,398	15,644	3,748	37.3	2,016	349	5.8	1,747	46.6	2,001
Idaho..............	12,797	1,270	7,918	2,945	43.1	1,884	194	9.7	1,464	49.7	1,481
Wyoming...........	3,795	1,375	12,946	4,243	32.4	2,076	451	4.6	1,826	43.0	2,417
Colorado...........	25,932	1,224	9,172	3,552	34.5	1,982	397	5.0	1,621	45.6	1,931
Utah...............	13,094	1,106	15,645	3,662	30.2	1,869	349	5.3	1,455	39.7	2,207
FAR WEST..........	470,443	1,273	8,416	3,331	38.2	2,051	332	6.2	1,605	48.2	1,726
Washington.........	101,260	1,269	6,672	2,916	43.5	2,044	263	7.8	1,532	52.5	1,384
Oregon.............	65,982	1,205	5,504	2,562	47.0	2,081	222	9.3	1,427	55.7	1,135
California..........	302,189	1,288	9,596	3,612	35.7	2,050	379	5.4	1,667	46.2	1,945
Nevada.............	1,012	1,461	20,324	10,800	13.5	1,736	429	4.0	1,890	17.5	8,910

CHAPTER II

MANUFACTURING FOR THE NATION—
GROUP I INDUSTRIES

The eleven southeastern states have 21.5 percent of the nation's population according to preliminary figures of the 1940 census. Roughly speaking, therefore, when more than that proportion of an industry is located in the Southeast, the region may be said to be manufacturing for the national market. There are, of course, many chances of error in using this rough measure: differences in the degree of mechanization and of skill in management make for differences in efficiency; differences in climate, occupations, customs and habits result in wide variations in the use of certain articles; differences in purchasing power probably result in even more. Within the limitations of this measure, there are some 44 industries (out of 352 into which the census separates manufacturing in the United States) in which 21.5 percent or more (measured by number of wage earners) is located in the Southeast.[1] In 22 of these industries it is possible to calculate with fair accuracy the proportion, not only of wage earners, but wages, value of product and value added by manufacture which is located in the Southeast. In the other 22 industries the reckoning is less accurate; due to regulations concerning disclosure of operations of individual establishments data for many states are grouped together. It is possible in some cases to make fairly accurate estimates from supplementary data on number of wage earners in the several states. There are a few others besides these 44 in which a sizeable proportion is in the Southeast, but for these it is impossible to make any reasonably accurate estimate.

It will be observed that nearly all these industries are based directly or indirectly on some crop or natural resource either peculiar to the Southeast or found more plentifully in that region than in other parts of the country. Partial exceptions are: distilled liquors, chiefly made in Kentucky and probably from grains not raised in the Southeast; rayon manufacture made partly from cotton linters but partly also from imported or northern wood or wood pulp; the succeeding process, rayon woven goods; and hosiery in the part of the industry using silk yarn.

[1] For list of the industries see table at end of chapter.

It would appear, therefore, that the Southeast is fulfilling the first rule for optimum production in regard to many of its special products and natural resources. Most of the direct, or first, processing furnishes employment for many producers on farm, in mine, or forest. In addition most of these products are made from raw materials which are bulky in relation to value; the processing requires no skills that are not common in the Southeast, easily acquired by training, or readily imported in the person of the few technical experts. The products are rendered considerably more valuable in proportion to bulk and more easily transportable. Nearly all are industries in which capital necessary for a workable unit is not large. There are a few in which it is very large, namely, cast iron pipe, rayon, sugar refining and pulp. The presence of these and of some large units in cigarettes, cotton goods, dyeing and finishing for example, proves that the region can either supply capital or get it from the outside when necessary.

SOUTHEASTERN MONOPOLY INDUSTRIES

These factors are particularly true of the top three, turpentine and rosin, cane sugar production, and cigarettes, in the manufacture of which the South has a virtual monopoly.

Cigarettes. Economically speaking the concentration of cigarette manufacture in the South is an almost perfect example of optimum production in Group I. It furnishes a market for a large crop for which a quarter of a million southern farmers receive more income than any other. There are short hauls of raw material, often a block or two by truck from the marketing floor to the factory or storage warehouse. The processing gives employment to a sizeable group of workers, over 26,000 in the nation of whom nearly 25,000 are in three southern states, North Carolina, Virginia, and Kentucky. This is a large enough number to be an important and valuable factor in those states and especially in the cities in which it is concentrated. Some 40 percent are Negroes, including many Negro women to whom relatively few lines of industrial employment are open. The wage per wage earner is $925. To be sure this is $255 less than the average for all industry in the United States ($1,180) but it is $166 more than the average for all industry in the Southeast ($759). Considering that practically all the industry is in the South where all wages are low, that it employs many unskilled workers, Negroes, women, and automatic machine tenders, it ranks rather high on this score. Even with internal revenue taxes deducted the value of product per wage earner is $17,500, a figure which places it in the top 10 percent among the 352 industries, and fifth from the top among industries employing over 20,000 workers.

Cigarette manufacture is one of the few industries in the South which completes the process of manufacture for the ultimate consumer instead of a few of the early, least skilled, least profitable stages. The value added by manufacture is $7,549 per wage earner. This places it seventeenth from the top among the 352 industries and it employs more workers than any of the other sixteen. Wages and salaries absorb $1,067 or 14.1 percent of the value added by manufacture. Book value of capital assets of the six largest tobacco companies[2] reporting in Moody's *Industrials* average $13,000 per wage earner. The large investment in tangibles—buildings, etc. and stocks of tobacco—make the industry a fruitful source of tax revenue to state and local governments. Since ownership of the stock is widely scattered it is true that only a part of the dividends remain in the South, but the building of the industry has meant bringing capital to the South, the reinvestment of earned surpluses in the South, and so an ever larger market for raw tobacco and employment for labor. The difference between the value of product and the value added by manufacture, $17,500 and $7,549 respectively per wage earner, is a rough measure of the amount of raw material, supplies, etc., which the industry uses. Besides the raw tobacco the cigarette industry is a sizeable user of electric power and a great user of "findings." Recently it has begun to build up in the South the accessory industries to supply some of these findings, such as tin foil and fine cigarette paper. It spends much money for paper products for containers, and for printing. All of these belong among the high index industries. It distributes a share of its advertising dollar in southern newspapers, and it advertises the South with every advertisement and every package. Although cigarettes are luxury products they sell in small units and thus are a luxury for the masses, one the consumption of which the people may lessen but rarely discontinue during hard times. Thus the industry is not as much affected by depression as are other luxuries and many necessities.

CIGARETTES	United States	Southeast	Percent
Number of wage earners	26,149	24,762	94.7
Wage per wage earner	$ 925	$ 922	99.7
Value of product per wage earner	$17,500*	$17,358*	99.2
Value added by manufacture per wage earner	$ 7,549	$ 7,696	101.9
Percent wages are of value added by manufacture	12.2	12.0	
Salary per salaried person	$ 2,459	$ 2,455	99.8
Salary per wage earner	$ 142	$ 138	97.2
Number of wage earners per salaried person	17.4	17.7	101.7
Wage and salary per wage earner	$ 1,067	$ 1,060	99.3
Percent wage and salary are of value added by manufacture	14.1	13.8	
Balance for interest, profits, taxes	$ 6,482	$ 6,636	102.4

*Internal revenue tax deducted.

In addition to all these features an extra boon is the fact that the Federal Government receives about a half billion dollars a year in taxes

[2] Most of these make chewing and smoking tobacco and snuff as well as cigarettes. It is impossible to separate the assets for the different products.

on cigarettes, nearly $20,000 per wage earner. Further, the industry has been experiencing steady growth.

This economic paragon of industries has an Achilles' heel—the nature of the product. Crusades against the cigarette have so far met with little success but it is still somewhat vulnerable and especially so in national emergencies. And pending a successful drive for prohibition, cigarettes are always subject to new and higher taxation.

Cane Sugar Manufacture. The other southeastern monopoly industries make a widely different showing. Cane sugar manufacture furnishes a market for an important crop which is bulky and should be processed close to the fields; therefore, it is appropriate that 100 percent of the industry is located in Louisiana and Florida. The industry employs relatively few, 4,221, including many Negroes, on a highly seasonal basis varying from 1,700 in February to 10,500 in December. The wage per wage earner ($565 a year[3]) places it ninth from the lowest among all 352 industries into which the census divides manufacturing. This is less than half the average for the whole United States, and nearly $200 less than the average for all industries in the Southeast. Salary per salaried worker is only 62 percent of the average for all industries in the United States, and 67 percent of the average for all in the Southeast. The value of product per wage earner is high for the Southeast, being approximately the average for the United States ($7,090). But most of this is because of the fact that one worker handles much material; the value added by manufacture per wage earner is about the average for the region. Deduction of the small wage of $565 and the salary expenditure per wage earner, $197 (compared incidentally with $142 in cigarettes), leaves $1,233 out of which to pay interest on investment, profits, taxes, etc. However, capital costs per wage earner are apparently not heavy: book values of a few companies listed by Moody suggest that investment is probably around $2,500 per wage earner. Its main disadvantages, therefore, are its low wages and salaries.

CANE SUGAR MANUFACTURE	United States	Southeast
Number of wage earners	4,221	4,221
Wage per wage earner	$ 565	$ 565
Value of product per wage earner	$ 6,920	$ 6,920
Value added by manufacture per wage earner	$ 1,995	$ 1,995
Percent wages are of value added by manufacture	28.3	28.3
Salary per salaried person	$ 1,386	$ 1,386
Salary per wage earner	$ 197	$ 197
Number of wage earners per salaried person	7.1	7.1
Wage and salary per wage earner	$ 762	$ 762
Percent wage and salary are of value added by manufacture	38.2	38.2
Balance for interest, profits, taxes	$ 1,233	$ 1,233

[3] Calculated on a basis of average number throughout the year and thus representing full year workers.

The industry is growing rapidly, having more than doubled in wage earners and value of product, and quadrupled in value added by manufacture between 1925 and 1937. Most of this increase occurred after 1931, reflecting changes in national policy regarding importation of sugar.

A much more desirable industry for the Southeast is the next manufacturing process—cane sugar refining. This will be discussed later in the section on Southeastern Quota Industries.

Turpentine and Rosin. The turpentine and rosin industry is in many ways a parallel to sugar production. It uses a natural resource, a bulky forest product that is peculiar to the South. It gives employment to some 30,000 workers in the woods. But it employs only some 1,500 workers itself, largely Negro men. It pays the lowest wage per wage earner of any industry in the United States—$232. Salaries, too, are extremely small, averaging only $664 per salaried person. And yet it is such a small scale industry (993 establishments) and has such a large salaried personnel (1,308) that the expenditure for salaries per wage earner is more than three times the average for the Southeast. Thus the two, wages and salaries per wage earner, amount to $809 compared with $762 in sugar manufacture, and yet wage earners and salaried persons alike earn less even than in sugar production. These figures are the more amazing when compared with the value added by manufacture per wage earner, $4,220. This is 40 percent more than the national average ($2,938) and more than double the southeastern average ($1,987). No basis for estimates of capital costs is available, but unless a company owns large forest reserves —a possibility but not a necessity for the industry—they should not be high.

TURPENTINE AND ROSIN	United States	Southeast
Number of wage earners	1,506	1,506
Wage per wage earner	$ 232	$ 232
Value of product per wage earner	$19,273	$19,273
Value added by manufacture per wage earner	$ 4,220	$ 4,220
Percent wages are of value added by manufacture	5.5	5.5
Salary per salaried person	$ 664	$ 664
Salary per wage earner	$ 577	$ 577
Number of wage earners per salaried person	1.2	1.2
Wage and salary per wage earner	$ 809	$ 809
Percent wage and salary are of value added by manufacture	19.2	19.2
Balance for interest, profits, taxes	$ 3,411	$ 3,411

The product is only semimanufactured in the industry and does not reach the ultimate consumer without further processing. The Southeast should develop the industries which use its turpentine and rosin. One of the greatest uses is in the manufacture of paints and varnish; one for rosin is soap making. Indices for these will be reviewed in their proper places.

Thus in the case of two of the three products for which the South is most peculiarly suited, it stops with semimanufactured products that severely exploit two resources—soil and forest—and employ few workers at very poor wages.

SOUTHEASTERN MAJORITY INDUSTRIES

There are two industries in which the Southeast manufactures three-fourths of the national product: cotton yarn and thread, and cotton goods. As in the case of the three already discussed, these belong to Group I: a peculiar natural resource which the region should manufacture for the whole nation. It has taken a century of argument on the part of southern leaders and half a century of development for the South to achieve this status in the manufacture of its most famous crop. In the past these two industries have meant much to the South in employment, wages, salaries, dividends, profits, trade, town and city building. For a very complicated set of reasons—overproduction, competition, trade organization, competing fibers and fabrics, rapid style changes, etc.—both industries have spent nearly the whole of the last two decades in depression. Traditionally semiskilled, low-wage industries, they have remained so for these internal conditions. Therefore, by comparison with more profitable, more monopolistic, or better organized industries, they appear worse now than when they were the chief factory manufacturing.

Nevertheless these two industries fulfill several of the requirements for Group I: they process a local and regional crop which engages agricultural workers on nearly two million farms; they use large quantities of a second natural resource—water power; and they employ large numbers of wage earners, recruitable and easily trained from among the region's teaming ranks of even more poorly employed population.

Cotton Yarn and Thread. But they are low index industries by every measure. Cotton yarn and thread, to take the one that is older in the South, ranks as twenty-sixth industry from the bottom in the nation in wages per wage earner and is the largest of the twenty-six. The salary per salaried person compares favorably with the national average ($2,232). The industry is not, however, overweighted with salaried workers; rather the contrary: the salary per wage earner is only slightly more than one-fourth the national average of $317 per wage earner. This figure and the large number of wage earners per salaried person suggests that only the minimum necessary for direct administrative, supervisory, and clerical work are employed, and very few for testing and laboratory research so necessary in modern industry. In value added by manufacture cotton yarn and thread ranks nineteenth from the bottom in the nation and, as in the wages index, it is the largest among the nineteen. For the whole industry this figure is $1,224, for the Southeast alone, $1,108, an amount which does much to explain the low wage and salary per wage earner. Over 60 percent of the value added goes for wages and salaries, leaving only $486 for interest on investment, profits, dividends, taxes, etc. There are some other industries which pay out in wages and salaries as large or even larger proportions of the value added by manufacture. But none employs as many wage earners or has so substantial an investment in buildings and machinery (between $2,000 and $2,500 per wage earner); in few is the actual as well as the relative amount left for the other items so small.

Cotton yarn and thread	United States	South-east	Per-cent
Number of wage earners	86,206	67,674	78.5
Wage per wage earner	$ 659	$ 610	92.6
Value of product per wage earner	$ 3,023	$ 2,862	94.7
Value added by manufacture per wage earner	$ 1,224	$ 1,108	90.5
Percent wages are of value added by manufacture	53.8	55.1	
Salary per salaried person	$ 2,164	$ 2,155	99.6
Salary per wage earner	$ 79	$ 55	69.6
Number of wage earners per salaried person	27.4	39.1	142.7
Wage and salary per wage earner	$ 738	$ 665	90.1
Percent wage and salary are of value added by manufacture	60.2	60.1	
Balance for interest, profits, taxes	$ 486	$ 443	91.2

Cotton Woven Goods. About the only industry that makes so poor a showing by all these indices is the companion industry, cotton goods. Like cotton yarn and thread, this industry processes a southern crop, uses much electric power, employs a large number of workers and is an important factor in the economic life of four southeastern states. Like yarn it is low index in all items, and since it employs four times as many wage earners, its low wage affects many more people. In value added by manufacture the cotton goods industry is twenty-seventh from the lowest in the nation, and is much the largest industry among the twenty-seven. The relative proportion of total expenditures for wages and salaries is slightly higher than in yarn, leaving about the same balance for all other items. Capital per wage earner—according to the Textile Institute about $3,000—is higher in this industry than in yarn because the additional machinery is expensive and is bulky and heavy, requiring more space and more substantial buildings. Except for two small contract-shop industries in the clothing trade the number of wage earners per salaried persons is the greatest of any in the United States. Not only does it offer relatively

Cotton woven goods	United States	South-east	Per-cent
Number of wage earners	336,104	248,800	74.0
Wage per wage earner	$ 761	$ 729	95.8
Value of product per wage earner	$ 2,877	$ 2,881	100.1
Value added by manufacture per wage earner	$ 1,313	$ 1,277	97.2
Percent wages are of value added by manufacture	58.0	57.0	
Salary per salaried person	$ 2,406	$ 2,437	101.3
Salary per wage earner	$ 60	$ 52	86.7
Number of wage earners per salaried person	40.3	46.6	115.9
Wage and salary per wage earner	$ 821	$ 781	95.1
Percent wage and salary are of value added by manufacture	62.5	61.2	
Balance for interest, profits, taxes	$ 492	$ 496	100.8

little employment to white collar workers but has few professional and technical workers.

Both of these industries are growing in the Southeast, but declining in the nation as a whole. These few statistics seem to indicate that the Southeast should hardly make efforts to secure more cotton yarn or cloth mills or should wave flags when one is built. Any outside or local capital other than for modernization of existing mills should certainly be devoted to more likely industries. Both these industries produce a semifinished rather than a consumers' article. Much of the product of the cotton yarn industry is further processed in the Southeast in dyeing and finishing and in knitting industries, as is much of the cotton cloth in finishing and in cutting-up industries. Indices for these will be given in the section on Southeastern Quota Industries.

Besides the three industries, cane sugar production, turpentine and rosin, and cigarettes, in the manufacture of which the Southeast has a virtual monopoly, and cotton yarn and thread and cotton goods, in which it manufactures about three quarters of the national product, there are three other industries of which well over one-half, as measured by wage earners, are located in the Southeast. These are cottonseed oil (68 percent), rice cleaning and polishing (67 percent), and fertilizers (62.3 percent). Application of the same indices to these industries is also revealing.

Rice Cleaning and Polishing. Rice cleaning and polishing, like the preceding industries, is important as a processer of a great agricultural crop peculiar to the South, and one that engages many people in the fields of some 6,000 farms. The industry employs only 2,218 wage earners on a seasonal basis ranging from 1,400 in July to 3,000 in October. It is, therefore, not so important as an industry, but because the raw material is a bulky article of low value, it is in the interest of the national economy that it be processed as near the fields as possible. And so it is—all except one plant in Tennessee—in Arkansas, California, Louisiana, and Texas. It has only one disadvantage: wages are low for the whole industry and are even lower for that part located in the Southeast. In Texas the wage per wage earner is $728 while in California it is $1,254, more than the national average for all industries. Indeed, it is probably only because the abundance of cheap, unskilled labor makes it unnecessary to pay more that wages in the Southeast are not higher. Certainly the value added by manufacture would seem to make a higher wage possible. Thus in the Southeast the industry is devoting to wages something less than one-fifth of the value added by manufacture, whereas the average for all industries in the United States and in the Southeast as well, is about two-fifths. No data suggesting probable capital costs per wage earner are available, though it seems unlikely that these would be high.

Relative to wage earners, the number of salaried workers attached to the industry is very large and the expenditure for salaries per wage earner is almost as great as for wages. The industry increased its number of wage earners substantially between 1925 and 1937, but by other indices it shows either declines or very small increases.

Rice cleaning and polishing	United States	Southeast	Percent
Number of wage earners	2,218	1,486	67.0
Wage per wage earner	$ 611	$ 474	77.6
Value of product per wage earner	$21,124	$17,579	83.2
Value added by manufacture per wage earner	$ 3,623	$ 2,565	70.8
Percent wages are of value added by manufacture	16.9	18.5	
Salary per salaried person	$ 2,196	$ 2,010	91.5
Salary per wage earner	$ 557	$ 488	87.6
Number of wage earners per salaried person	3.9	4.1	105.1
Wage and salary per wage earner	$ 1,168	$ 962	82.4
Percent wage and salary are of value added by manufacture	32.2	37.4	
Balance for interest, profits, taxes	$ 2,455	$ 1,603	65.3

Cottonseed Oil, Cake and Meal. Cottonseed oil, cake and meal offers almost an exact parallel to rice cleaning and polishing: a bulky, cheap product and a seasonal industry using much unskilled labor. The industry is much larger, however, employing 16,500 wage earners of whom 11,259 are in the Southeast, with most of the remainder in Texas, Oklahoma, and California. It, also, is a very low wage industry. In value added by manufacture it is near the national average and well above the southeastern average for all industries. Its wage of less than one-fifth the value added by manufacture, suggests, therefore, as in the case of rice cleaning, that it might well pay more if necessary in order to secure labor. On the other hand, capital cost is fairly high, the limited data seeming to indicate it to be around $4,000 per wage earner. The industry has declined since 1925, and with cotton control programs and declining market for cotton in the air, it bids fair to continue this trend.

Cottonseed oil, meal, cake	United States	Southeast	Percent
Number of wage earners	16,583	11,259	68.0
Wage per wage earner	$ 514	$ 495	96.3
Value of product per wage earner	$14,596	$14,765	101.2
Value added by manufacture per wage earner	$ 2,792	$ 2,522	90.3
Percent wages are of value added by manufacture	18.4	19.6	
Salary per salaried person	$ 2,028	$ 2,063	101.7
Salary per wage earner	$ 341	$ 305	89.4
Number of wage earners per salaried person	6.0	6.8	113.3
Wage and salary per wage earner	$ 855	$ 800	93.6
Percent wage and salary are of value added by manufacture	30.6	31.7	
Balance for interest, profits, taxes	$ 1,937	$ 1,722	88.9

Incidentally cottonseed oil is the lowest wage and lowest but one in value added by manufacture among the great chemical group of industries. This industry is not in the South because it is a low index industry but because it naturally belongs in the South and because it carries on the first rough processing of an agricultural product. In this respect it is also a parallel of the sugar production industry: the Southeast carries on two-thirds of this first process and stops short of the valuable branch of the industry, processing crude oil into shortening and salad oils. This latter is a high index industry especially in its use of raw materials. It has been growing rapidly since 1933, the first year for which separate statistics are available. It will be discussed in Group II as an industry the region should encourage.

Fertilizers. In the chemical group, which is for the most part made up of high index industries, the one that ranks next lowest to cottonseed oil is fertilizers. Nearly two-thirds of its wage earners are in the Southeast. It is appropriate that so much should be in this region: most of the necessary raw materials are to be found in the area; the bulky materials and the equally bulky finished product require the shortest possible hauls; the Southeast is the greatest user of commercial fertilizers. With nearly 21,000 wage earners the industry is important as an employer of labor. A large proportion of these are unskilled, and in the Southeast are Negroes. It is highly seasonal, the number of workers ranging from nearly 37,000 in April to less than 15,000 in July. Indices of both wages and salaries are low compared with national and regional averages. The balance after these items are deducted is higher than average but this advantage is partly cancelled by the fact that capital costs are relatively high: average book values of assets in three large and three small companies amount to over $7,000 per wage earner. The industry has experienced decreases in all measures of size except wage earners since 1925.

Fertilizers	United States	Southeast	Percent
Number of wage earners	20,893	13,017	62.3
Wage per wage earner	$ 735	$ 539	73.3
Value of product per wage earner	$ 9,370	$ 8,608	91.9
Value added by manufacture per wage earner	$ 3,144	$ 2,660	84.6
Percent wages are of value added by manufacture	23.4	20.3	
Salary per salaried person	$ 1,902	$ 1,742	91.6
Salary per wage earner	$ 305	$ 271	88.8
Number of wage earners per salaried person	6.2	6.5	104.8
Wage and salary per wage earner	$ 1,040	$ 810	77.9
Percent wage and salary are of value added by manufacture	33.1	30.5	
Balance for interest, profits, taxes	$ 2,104	$ 1,850	87.9

Wood Distillation. There are a few other industries of which somewhat more than one-half are located in the Southeast, but because of rules regarding disclosure of data for individual plants, it is impossible to determine the exact proportion. One of these is wood distillation of which probably 68 percent is found in the Southeast. In Mississippi, which for this industry is the most important state in the region, the indices are well above those for the industry as a whole. It is growing rapidly, having increased 68.3 percent in wage earners, 128.5 percent in value of product and 198.4 percent in value added by manufacture since 1931, the first year for which separate figures are available. Inasmuch as its products are chemicals or are used in other chemical industries, this increase means more than mere recovery from the depression.

Wood distillation	United States	Mississippi	Percent
Number of wage earners	4,467	884	
Wage per wage earner	$ 901	$ 902	100.1
Value of product per wage earner	$ 5,853	$ 7,450	127.3
Value added by manufacture per wage earner	$ 3,317	$ 4,840	145.9
Percent wages are of value added by manufacture	27.1	18.7	
Salary per salaried person	$ 1,914	$ 2,123	110.9
Salary per wage earner	$ 239	$ 222	92.9
Number of wage earners per salaried person	8.0	9.6	120.0
Wage and salary per wage earner	$ 1,140	$ 1,124	98.6
Percent wage and salary are of value added by manufacture	34.4	23.3	
Balance for interest, profits, taxes	$ 2,177	$ 3,716	170.7

Cast Iron Pipe. Another example is the cast iron pipe industry of which probably 60 percent is located in the Southeast. This is the lowest index industry among the 28 in the iron and steel group, and the part in Alabama, the most important single state, is slightly lower than the industry as a whole. Wages and salaries per wage earner are low, but even so these expenditures leave less than $1,000 per wage earner for all other items. This is very small considering the capital investment necessary: five companies for which book values of assets are available, though showing wide variation among themselves, average about $6,500 per wage earner. The industry has decreased by all measures since 1925, in some as much as 40 percent. It may recover with increased building and city improvement.

Cast iron pipe	United States	Alabama	Percent
Number of wage earners	17,613	8,316	
Wage per wage earner	$ 1,027	$ 916	89.2
Value of product per wage earner	$ 3,470	$ 3,380	97.4
Value added by manufacture per wage earner	$ 2,026	$ 2,003	98.9
Percent wages are of value added by manufacture	50.6	45.8	
Salary per salaried person	$ 2,379	$ 2,332	98.0
Salary per wage earner	$ 164	$ 138	84.1
Number of wage earners per salaried person	14.5	16.9	116.6
Wage and salary per wage earner	$ 1,191	$ 1,054	88.5
Percent wage and salary are of value added by manufacture	58.8	52.6	
Balance for interest, profits, taxes	$ 835	$ 949	113.6

Thus of the 10 industries in which the Southeast specializes only 2 are found to be high in all counts. One of these, cigarettes, is already so completely in the region that expansion can proceed only as the industry grows. Expansion in the second, wood distillation, appears possible and desirable; this seems to be a more promising way of utilizing forest resources than the older types of wood using industries, but it is a small industry.

SOUTHEASTERN QUOTA INDUSTRIES

There are 34 industries in which the actual or estimated number of wage earners in the Southeast range from 20 to 50 percent of the total engaged in the industry. In all of these the region is, on a basis of population and perhaps even more so on a basis of consumption, manufacturing for the nation.

Lumber and Timber Products. A number of these center around the forest resources of the region. The largest, lumber and timber products, is an important industry in the Southeast. It is widespread, its 3,744 establishments in the region touching thousands of communities, and furnishing a market for timber and a supply of building materials convenient to all. But the wage per wage earner is low, distressingly so considering the fact that the workers are practically all men in the prime of their working life. The value added by manufacture per wage earner is so low that the small wage and salary per wage earner leaves only $496 for all other items. To be sure it does not require great investment unless a company owns large forest reserves, but the above amount for interest, etc. places it in the class with some types of mining as an exploiter of a natural resource. The industry has declined 30 percent in number of wage earners, and 40 percent in value of products and value added by manufacture since 1925: with a revival of building it may regain its old position, but in the long run it appears doomed to decrease for lack of raw materials.

LUMBER AND TIMBER PRODUCTS	United States	Southeast	Percent
Number of wage earners	323,928	144,124	44.5
Wage per wage earner	$ 849	$ 532	62.7
Value of product per wage earner	$ 2,619	$ 1,955	74.6
Value added by manufacture per wage earner	$ 1,555	$ 1,120	72.0
Percent wages are of value added by manufacture	54.6	47.5	
Salary per salaried person	$ 2,166	$ 2,043	94.3
Salary per wage earner	$ 107	$ 92	86.0
Number of wage earners per salaried person	20.2	22.1	109.4
Wage and salary per wage earner	$ 956	$ 624	65.3
Percent wage and salary are of value added by manufacture	61.5	55.7	
Balance for interest, profits, taxes	$ 599	$ 496	82.8

Wooden Boxes. Several of the other industries in the list are really employed in further processing of the products of the lumber and timber industry. The Southeast has two-fifths of the wage earners in the wooden box industry. This has lower indices than lumber and timber. Its lower actual balance for interest, etc. is relatively better since capital investment is not as high. This industry has decreased since 1925 in about the same

WOODEN BOXES (EXCEPT CIGAR)	United States	Southeast	Percent
Number of wage earners	25,981	10,298	39.6
Wage per wage earner	$ 752	$ 498	66.2
Value of product per wage earner	$ 3,323	$ 2,124	63.9
Value added by manufacture per wage earner	$ 1,574	$ 1,058	67.2
Percent wages are of value added by manufacture	47.8	47.1	
Salary per salaried person	$ 2,244	$ 2,304	102.7
Salary per wage earner	$ 172	$ 105	61.0
Number of wage earners per salaried person	13.1	22.0	167.9
Wage and salary per wage earner	$ 924	$ 603	65.2
Percent wage and salary are of value added by manufacture	58.7	57.0	
Balance for interest, profits, taxes	$ 650	$ 455	70.0

proportions as lumber and timber. It will probably decrease more as lumber increases in cost and as substitutes come into even more general use.

Planing Mill Products. The region has 28.2 percent of the total wage earners in the planing mill products industry. This requires considerably more skilled workers and is, therefore, better than lumber and timber, but it is below the regional average in all indices. Figures for 1925 are not comparable, but in nearly every state in which this is an important industry it has shown sharp declines since 1929.[4]

Planing mill products	United States	South-east	Per-cent
Number of wage earners	66,814	18,810	28.2
Wage per wage earner	$ 1,014	$ 702	69.2
Value of product per wage earner	$ 4,678	$ 3,850	82.3
Value added by manufacture per wage earner	$ 2,062	$ 1,516	73.5
Percent wages are of value added by manufacture	49.1	46.4	
Salary per salaried person	$ 1,988	$ 1,818	91.4
Salary per wage earner	$ 296	$ 201	67.9
Number of wage earners per salaried person	6.7	9.1	135.8
Wage and salary per wage earner	$ 1,310	$ 903	68.9
Percent wage and salary are of value added by manufacture	63.5	59.6	
Balance for interest, profits, taxes	$ 752	$ 613	81.5

Miscellaneous Wood Industries. There are five smaller wood using industries of which the Southeast has from 39 to 23 percent of the wage earners. Baskets and willow ware is one of the lowest index industries in the United States, the regional differential bringing the wage in Virginia, the principal southeastern state, to $313 and a balance, after deduction of wages and salaries, of $243. Cooperage, though considerably better, is much lower than national or even southeastern averages for all industries. Of the wooden cigar boxes and excelsior the same may be said and in addition they are industries which show indications of declining in the future. In wood, turned and shaped, the indices are low but at least are better than for lumber and timber. This industry has grown considerably in several southeastern states since 1929.[5]

Furniture. Furniture makes a better showing in wages, being at least up to the regional average for all industries. But the value added by manu-

Furniture (household and office)	United States	South-east	Per-cent
Number of wage earners	170,072	38,538	22.6
Wage per wage earner	$ 1,015	$ 758	74.7
Value of product per wage earner	$ 3,870	$ 3,080	79.6
Value added by manufacture per wage earner	$ 2,060	$ 1,505	73.0
Percent wages are of value added by manufacture	49.3	50.4	
Salary per salaried person	$ 2,149	$ 2,249	104.6
Salary per wage earner	$ 243	$ 157	64.6
Number of wage earners per salaried person	8.8	14.3	162.5
Wage and salary per wage earner	$ 1,258	$ 915	72.7
Percent wage and salary are of value added by manufacture	61.0	60.5	
Balance for interest, profits, taxes	$ 812	$ 590	72.7

[4] *Monthly Labor Review,* Volume 50, pp. 1330-1339, June, 1940.
[5] *Ibid.* For indices of these five industries see table at end of chapter.

facture per wage earner is well below the regional average, and the balance for interest, etc. on an estimated capital per wage earner of about $3,000 is only $590. The industry in 1937 showed a decline from 1925 of 6 percent in wage earners, 24 percent in value of product and 27 percent in value added by manufacture.

Wood Preserving. Wood preserving is about average, and the portion of the industry in Mississippi, the chief southeastern state, is so much more promising than most wood using industries that it probably warrants encouragement. It has increased nearly 200 percent since 1933, when the first figures were secured on this as a separate industry. It will probably continue to grow since it supplies the increasing demand for woods treated for protection against decay and insects.[6]

Pulp. From the above discussion it would appear that the Southeast is exploiting one of its great natural resources—forests—on a basis of subsistence wages to workers and extremely small returns to capital. It could much better turn those woods which are suitable into pulp and paper. The pulp industry employed 26,994 workers in 1937 of which the Southeast had approximately 25 percent. It is a high index industry, even in the Southeast; the indices for Virginia, the chief state in the region, approach, and by some measure surpass the national average for all industries. Only two-fifths of the value added by manufacture is required for wages and salaries compared with 51 percent for all industries. Therefore, though capital investment per wage earner is high—the average of capital assets of a dozen companies in Moody's amounting to over $11,000 per wage earner—the balance furnishes a liberal amount for interest, profits, taxes, etc. Moreover, it is a growing industry, with 33.5 percent more wage earners than in 1925, and 48 percent greater value of product. The paper industry has even higher indices. Since the Southeast has less than 20 percent of the wage earners in paper manufacture this will be discussed in Group II (p. 43).

PULP	United States	Virginia	Percent
Number of wage earners	26,994	1,823	
Wage per wage earner	$ 1,244	$ 1,090	87.6
Value of product per wage earner	$ 9,157	$ 9,950	108.7
Value added by manufacture per wage earner	$ 3,465	$ 3,160	91.2
Percent wages are of value added by manufacture	35.9	34.5	
Salary per salaried person	$ 2,392	$ 2,790	116.6
Salary per wage earner	$ 191	$ 219	114.6
Number of wage earners per salaried person	12.5	12.7	101.6
Wage and salary per wage earner	$ 1,435	$ 1,309	91.2
Percent wage and salary are of value added by manufacture	41.4	41.3	
Balance for interest, profits, taxes	$ 2,030	$ 1,851	91.2

Paper Bags. The Southeast has about one-fourth of the 10,360 wage earners in paper bag manufacture. While a considerably lower wage industry than pulp or paper, it is average in other respects and is in general

[6] For indices see table at end of chapter.

better than most industries in the region. Since the popularity of paper as a container is increasing it is likely to continue the growth it has registered since 1933.[7]

Tanning Materials. Another small industry, classified in the chemical group, but based largely on forest products is tanning materials, mordants, etc. This is a high index industry in all respects except wages.[8]

Rayon and Allied Products. Also in the chemical group and partly based on forest products is rayon and allied products. Rayon has been the miracle fiber of the twentieth century. Between 1925 and 1937 the industry increased about threefold. It ranks high by every measure, and the indices for Virginia, the southeastern state with most wage earners, are even higher than for the industry as a whole. Capital investment is considerable, the average per wage earner for seven companies amounting to $5,500 and large units are necessary for practicable operation. The fact that the Southeast has nearly half of the industry shows that even large amounts of capital can be raised or attracted to the region for advantageous industries.

RAYON AND ALLIED PRODUCTS	United States	Virginia	Percent
Number of wage earners	55,098	10,637	
Wage per wage earner	$ 1,185	$ 1,220	103.0
Value of product per wage earner	$ 4,623	$ 5,252	113.6
Value added by manufacture per wage earner	$ 3,159	$ 3,600	117.1
Percent wages are of value added by manufacture	37.5	33.0	
Salary per salaried person	$ 2,239	$ 2,482	110.8
Salary per wage earner	$ 210	$ 258	122.8
Number of wage earners per salaried person	10.6	9.6	90.6
Wage and salary per wage earner	$ 1,395	$ 1,478	105.9
Percent wage and salary are of value added by manufacture	44.2	40.0	
Balance for interest, profits, taxes	$ 1,764	$ 2,122	126.0

Rayon Woven Goods. The weaving of the fiber, however, has taken on many of the characteristics of its cousin, cotton. Thus the rayon woven goods industry has almost as low indices as cotton goods. Comparison of the following figures with those for rayon in the preceding table is illuminating.

RAYON WOVEN GOODS	United States	Southeast	Percent
Number of wage earners	57,949	20,865	36.0
Wage per wage earner	$ 845	$ 794	94.0
Value of product per wage earner	$ 3,965	$ 3,806	96.0
Value added by manufacture per wage earner	$ 1,391	$ 1,279	91.9
Percent wages are of value added by manufacture	60.8	62.1	
Salary per salaried person	$ 2,160	$ 1,994	91.9
Salary per wage earner	$ 91	$ 57	62.6
Number of wage earners per salaried person	23.7	35.0	147.7
Wage and salary per wage earner	$ 936	$ 851	90.9
Percent wage and salary are of value added by manufacture	67.2	66.6	
Balance for interest, profits, taxes	$ 455	$ 428	94.1

[7] For indices see table at end of chapter.
[8] *Ibid.*

Rayon weavery is increasing, particularly in the Southeast.[9] With 35 wage earners per salaried person it offers little employment to white collar workers; with only $428 balance for interest, profits, taxes, etc. it gains chiefly because the capital investment required is even smaller than for cotton goods and because the new fiber is displacing silk.

Hosiery. In 10 other textile industries the Southeast manufactures for the nation. All these industries process further the cotton yarn and cotton woven goods already discussed. The largest of these is hosiery. About 60 percent of all hosiery, by value, is of other fibers than cotton, and it is impossible to secure state or regional production by fibers from the census. But even with silk hosiery included, the indices for the whole industry are low.

HOSIERY	United States	South-east	Per-cent
Number of wage earners	150,460	66,458	44.2
Wage per wage earner	$ 906	$ 714	78.8
Value of product per wage earner	$ 2,403	$ 2,137	88.9
Value added by manufacture per wage earner	$ 1,340	$ 1,109	82.8
Percent wages are of value added by manufacture	67.6	64.5	
Salary per salaried person	$ 2,236	$ 2,321	103.8
Salary per wage earner	$ 100	$ 78	78.0
Number of wage earners per salaried person	22.2	29.5	132.9
Wage and salary per wage earner	$ 1,006	$ 792	78.6
Percent wage and salary are of value added by manufacture	75.2	71.5	
Balance for interest, profits, taxes	$ 334	$ 317	95.2

Some idea of the difference between silk and cotton hosiery can be obtained by comparing individual states. In general the part of the industry in Indiana and Pennsylvania, for example, is silk full-fashioned. Some of that in North Carolina is cotton, some silk full-fashioned. Most of that in South Carolina and Georgia is cotton. The following figures show the differences:

	Wage per wage earner	Value added by manufacture per wage earner	Balance
South Carolina	$ 680	$ 898	$218
Georgia	596	1,060	464
North Carolina	792	1,206	414
Pennsylvania	1,080	1,455	375
Indiana	1,175	1,855	710

The part of the industry making full-fashioned silk hosiery has been growing rapidly in the last decade and much of the expansion has taken place in the Southeast. Some of this regional growth has been by actual removal from the Northeast. The figures above show why part of this movement has been from Pennsylvania. The better wages it has brought are a great boon to many towns and cities in Virginia, North Carolina, and Tennessee. It is doubtful, however, if the gains involved in the acquisition

[9] *Monthly Labor Review, loc. cit.*

of an industry so low in wealth producing ability offset, from the point of view of regional or national well-being, the disturbance it creates in the economy of the states losing it. If the new fiber, nylon, lives up to its early promises of greater durability the present productive capacity of the hosiery industry will be too large.

Knitted Underwear. The Southeast also processes yarn into knitted underwear, having about one-third of the wage earners. This, too, is a low index industry. The balance left for other purposes than wages and salaries is only $436 in the Southeast and, though it is not an industry requiring large investment, this balance is none too promising—less than half the average of all industries in the region. The industry has experienced severe declines since 1925.

Knitted underwear	United States	Southeast	Percent
Number of wage earners	39,923	13,276	33.3
Wage per wage earner	$ 715	$ 647	90.5
Value of product per wage earner	$ 2,950	$ 2,650	89.8
Value added by manufacture per wage earner	$ 1,361	$ 1,177	86.5
Percent wages are of value added by manufacture	52.5	55.0	
Salary per salaried person	$ 2,157	$ 2,262	104.9
Salary per wage earner	$ 144	$ 94	65.3
Number of wage earners per salaried person	15.0	24.1	160.7
Wage and salary per wage earner	$ 859	$ 741	86.3
Percent wage and salary are of value added by manufacture	63.0	63.0	
Balance for interest, profits, taxes	$ 502	$ 436	86.8

Dyeing and Finishing. The Southeast carries further the processing of much of its yarn and cloth in the dyeing and finishing industries. Although these, too, are low index industries, they are considerably better than spinning and weaving.[10] The individual states vary greatly, especially in the matter of value added by manufacture per wage earner: Georgia, $1,230, South Carolina, $1,570, and North Carolina, $2,660. The reason for the high index in North Carolina is probably because two of the largest finishers carry the process through to the completed towels, sheets and pillow cases. The conclusion is obvious: planning groups might include dyeing and finishing among industries to be encouraged; they would do better to foster the complete finishing process. It must be admitted, however, that these industries as a whole have experienced decreases since 1925.

Cordage and Twine. The cordage and twine industry as a whole has much higher indices than its closely related industry, cotton yarn. But in the chief state in the Southeast, Georgia, it falls below the values in the yarn industry.[11]

Cotton Cutting-up Industries. The Southeast has begun to make some of its cloth into clothing and other articles. During the depression factories making cheap cotton garments were hard pressed in states with high labor standards or high wage levels. Many came to the Southeast upon

---

[10] Indices given in table at end of chapter. [11] Indices given in table at end of chapter.

their own initiative or upon invitation of, or with inducements from, southern towns eager for some sort of pay rolls. Many moved on when free rent, free electric power, or other inducements ceased.

On the face of it a good case can be made for the further development of these factories in the Southeast. They use a semifinished product made in the same state, and often in the same town with the weaving factory; they process it for ultimate consumers many of whom are in the immediate neighborhood or at least the region; they employ large numbers of women on jobs for which training can be done quickly. But the application of the simple indices used in this study to a few of those industries throws an entirely different light on these usually sound arguments. The dozen cutting-up industries using exclusively or predominantly cotton goods are among the twenty lowest wage industries of all the 352 in the United States and, of course, that portion of each industry in the Southeast shows even lower wages per wage earner. For example, in the case of men's and boy's work and sport clothing (including work shirts), for which it is possible to calculate a regional average, the wage per wage earner in the Southeast is only $481 compared with $594 for the whole industry. Regional figures for others cannot be secured, but comparison for individual states can be made: in the case of wash trousers, the wage per wage earner for the whole industry is $603, but is only $436 in Georgia, $450 in Louisiana, and $462 in Virginia. In the case of shirts (not work), etc. the wage per wage earner for the industry is $629, but it is $568 in Georgia, $382 in North Carolina, $444 in South Carolina and $367 in Virginia.

Nor is the case any better if the value added by manufacture is considered. These same dozen cutting-up industries fall among the lowest thirty in the nation. The men's and boys' work clothing industry shows a value added of only $1,029 for the United States and $788 for the part of it in the Southeast. In the case of wash trousers the value added for the whole industry is $1,081; in Georgia it is $584. Bags other than paper, and curtains and draperies are a little better, but for the part in the Southeast, not much better. None of these industries requires large capital investment, the average for many cotton garment industries being estimated at around $1,000. But the balance for interest, etc. in sample states ranges as low as $90.[12]

Industries with wages and value creating ability so low are parasitic industries. Their workers must depend partially on someone else for support, just as their managements must depend on public subsidy, concessions of some sort or relaxation of standards. With all these concessions many individual companies go into bankruptcy. Three or four of the largest of these industries have grown rapidly in the Southeast in recent

[12] Indices for these cotton cutting-up industries in table at end of chapter.

years. It is questionable, even for the sake of the temporary pay rolls they bring, whether they are an advantage to a town, a state, or a region. Certainly no planned development should include them until the public is willing to pay enough for its cotton clothing to make the industry self-supporting.

Cane Sugar Refining. In only a few of the food and kindred products group does the Southeast manufacture for the nation. One industry, cane sugar refining, was referred to in the discussion of the "monopoly" group as contrasting with the preceding process, cane sugar manufacture. This is a high index industry and the part in the Southeast rises well above average on all scores except wages which could, no doubt, be higher if necessary. For, although investment is high—possibly as much as $10,000 per wage earner—the balance for interest, etc. is about double the national average. Of course industry as a whole refines much sugar imported in a semifinished state. The Southeast may, and certainly should, refine all the sugar that it raises and manufactures, in order to perform the more profitable part of the whole process. With ports near the West Indies production areas the region is even more conveniently reached by water transportation than the northeastern states. On the other hand the industry has experienced declines since 1925. Expansion in the Southeast as elsewhere probably waits on better markets.

CANE SUGAR REFINING	United States	Louisiana	Percent
Number of wage earners	14,024	3,181	
Wage per wage earner	$ 1,140	$ 700	61.4
Value of product per wage earner	$30,200	$23,630	78.2
Value added by manufacture per wage earner	$ 4,410	$ 3,560	80.7
Percent wages are of value added by manufacture	25.8	19.7	
Salary per salaried person	$ 2,340	$ 1,814	77.5
Salary per wage earner	$ 283	$ 135	47.7
Number of wage earners per salaried person	8.3	13.3	160.2
Wage and salary per wage earner	$ 1,423	$ 835	58.7
Percent wage and salary are of value added by manufacture	32.2	23.4	
Balance for interest, profits, taxes	$ 2,987	$ 2,725	91.2

Beverages, Nonalcoholic. Nonalcoholic beverages are similar to cigarettes—a cheap luxury for the masses and one that is extremely popular in the Southeast. The patents for one of the most popular are owned in the region. It is not surprising, therefore, to find that the Southeast has 30 percent of the wage earners in the industry. The wage per wage earner for the region is well above the regional average for all industries. The value added by manufacture is actually higher in the Southeast than for the entire industry, one of the few industries in which this is true. Although the capital investment is high—the nine largest companies average over $7,000 per wage earner in book value of assets—the balance for interest, profits, taxes is also large. Financially, then, it is a desirable industry, and one that is growing rapidly (85 percent increase in wage earners and 148.7 percent in value of product between 1933 and 1937). With less than five wage earners per salaried person, it offers relatively numerous opportunities for technical and clerical workers.

BEVERAGES, NONALCOHOLIC	United States	Southeast	Percent
Number of wage earners	27,979	8,466	30.4
Wage per wage earner	$ 1,107	$ 963	87.0
Value of product per wage earner	$ 9,892	$10,540	106.6
Value added by manufacture per wage earner	$ 5,876	$ 6,149	104.6
Percent wages are of value added by manufacture	18.8	15.7	
Salary per salaried person	$ 2,301	$ 2,646	115.0
Salary per wage earner	$ 552	$ 565	102.4
Number of wage earners per salaried person	4.2	4.6	109.5
Wage and salary per wage earner	$ 1,659	$ 1,528	92.1
Percent wage and salary are of value added by manufacture	28.3	25.0	
Balance for interest, profits, taxes	$ 4,217	$ 4,621	109.6

Distilled Liquor. The Southeast has a third of the wage earners in the distilled liquor industry, practically all of whom are in Kentucky. The indices of this industry are very similar to those for nonalcoholic beverages.[13]

Manufactured Ice. The Southeast has 26 percent of the wage earners in the manufactured ice industry. The southeastern indices of the industry are well above those for all industry in the region. But this is a static, if not an actually declining, industry.[14]

Canned and Cured Fish, etc. On the basis of geography alone it is rather surprising that the Southeast has only about a fourth of the canned and cured fish industry. One of the often noted assets of the Southeast is its long coast line and many sounds, bays, and coves, all, to hear the boasting, teeming with fish. If the portion of the industry in the Southeast is able to pay a wage per wage earner of only $284 and produce a value added by manufacture of only $905, then the Southeast would better sell its fish, oysters, etc., uncanned. They could hardly return less in that form and at least a lot of uncomfortable, raw, cold, dirty work could be avoided.[15]

Lime and Stone Cutting. The lime industry, of which apparently about one-fourth is located in the Southeast, ranks almost as a median industry by its national indices; those for Virginia, the chief state in the region, are low even for the Southeast.[16] Like lime, the cutting and shaping of marble, granite, and other stones is another industry based on one of the boasted natural resources of the South. The wage per wage earner in the portion located in the Southeast is $876. This is $117 higher than the average for all industries in the region, but it is very low for an industry employing all men, about half of whom are highly skilled workers. The value added per wage earner is $1,930, less than the average for all industry

[13] For indices see table at end of chapter. [14] *Ibid.*
[15] *Ibid.* [16] *Ibid.*

INDUSTRIES WITH LOWEST WAGES PER WAGE EARNER
Fifty-four Industries With Wages Per Wage Earner Less Than $800

Industry	Number of wage earners	Wages per wage earner		Percent of wage earners in Southeast
Jute goods...	6,522	$ 796		?
Silk broad woven goods...................................	17,597	796		12.0 cir
Feathers and plumes......................................	559	782		No data by states
Gloves and mittens, leather...............................	11,637	777		0
Jewelry and instrument cases..............................	4,788	771		No data by states
Buttons..	12,026	770		4.0 cir
Clothing, women's and misses', not elsewhere classified....	26,897	766		1.0 cir
Cotton woven goods over 12 inches.........................	336,104	761	729	74.0
Excelsior..	960	760		23.0 cir
Leather goods, small articles.............................	2,443	757		0
Flags, banners, regalia, etc..............................	2,146	756		1.0 cir
Suspenders, garters, etc..................................	2,903	755		1.0 cir
Knitted outerwear, contract factories.....................	2,715	755		0
Boxes, wooden, except cigar...............................	25,981	752	498	39.6
Silk yarn and thread (for sale)...........................	10,572	740		7.0 cir
Fertilizers..	20,893	735	539	62.3
Knitted underwear..	39,923	715	647	33.3
Brooms...	4,067	714	525	18.4
Curtains, draperies, bedspreads, contract factories.......	711	712		0
Boxes, cigar...	3,296	704		26.0 cir
Furnishing, goods, men's, contract factories..............	759	703		0
Rayon yarn, processed for sale............................	5,399	677		11.0 cir
Artificial and preserved flowers..........................	5,657	688		No data by states
Canned and dried fruits, vegetables, pickles, etc.........	137,064	676	357	11.3
Cigars...	55,879	671		22.0 cir
Gloves and mittens, knitted...............................	3,182	667		0
Poultry dressing and packing..............................	8,913	666		4.0 cir
Curtains, draperies and bedspreads........................	8,934	661		20.0 cir
Cotton yarn and thread....................................	86,206	659	610	78.5
Rag carpets and rugs.....................................	429	654		2.0 cir
Blouses, women's and misses, contract factories...........	2,554	650		0
Outerwear, children's, contract factories.................	5,157	641		3.0 cir
Clothing, women's and misses, not elsewhere classified, cont. factories..	5,178	638		0
Men's and boys' shirts (except work), collars, nightwear, reg. factories	55,570	629		13.0 cir
Handkerchiefs, contract factories.........................	932	629		0
Underwear, women's and children's, knitted................	10,453	628		4.0 cir
Handkerchiefs, regular factories..........................	4,065	627		10.0 cir
Underwear, women's and children's woven...................	8,835	624		2.0 cir
Gloves, cloth or cloth and leather........................	12,679	619		9.0 cir
Rayon throwing and spinning, commission...................	1,937	615		0
Rice cleaning and polishing...............................	2,218	611	474	67.0
Dresses, house, uniform, etc., regular factories..........	28,250	608		1.0 cir
Men's and boys' trousers, wash suits......................	15,817	603		25.0 cir
Men's and boys' work and sport clothes....................	69,502	594	481	35.3
Silk throwing and spinning, (commission only).............	13,290	586		4.0 cir
Cane sugar production....................................	4,221	565	565	100.0
Baskets, willow ware, etc................................	9,308	551		39.0 cir
Dresses, house, uniforms, etc., contract factories........	4,039	545		1.0 cir
Men's and boys' underwear, regular factories..............	7,888	534		18.0 cir
Cotton seed oil, cake and meal............................	16,583	514	495	68.0
Men's and boys' shirts (except work), contract factories..	12,024	508		1.0 cir
Canned and cured fish, etc................................	18,229	478	284	26.0
Men's and boys' underwear, contract factories.............	1,424	437		0
Turpentine and rosin.....................................	1,506	232	232	100.0

Bold-faced figures indicate wages per wage earner in the Southeast.

in the Southeast.[17] While this industry does not require as heavy investment in buildings and machinery as many manufactures, it does require considerable capital for reserves in quarry holdings. This seems to be another case where the Southeast is exploiting a natural resource on a marginal basis. This industry, like all those producing building materials, has suffered serious decreases from 1925. The most promising of the manufactures based on mineral resources is the small ground minerals and earths industry. This has relatively high indices in Georgia, the chief southeastern state.[18]

Tobacco. The two remaining industries of Group I are cigars and chewing and smoking tobacco and snuff. The first, cigars, largely concentrated in Florida, is a low index industry.[19] The other, a factory process,

[17] For indices see table at end of chapter.   [18] *Ibid.*   [19] *Ibid.*

MANUFACTURING FOR THE NATION

Industries With Lowest Value Added by Manufacture Per Wage Earner

Forty-six Industries With Value Added Per Wage Earner of Less Than $1,600

Industry	Number of wage earners	Value added by manufacture per wage earner	Southeast value added per wage earner	Percent of wage earners in Southeast
Boxes, wooden, except cigar	25,981	$1,574	**1,058**	39.6
Lumber and timber products	323,928	1,555	**1,120**	44.5
Jewelry and instrument cases	4,788	1,534		No data by states
Women's and misses' coats and suits, contract factories	18,923	1,529		0
Typewriters and parts	21,440	1,474		0
Buttons	12,026	1,473		4.0 cir
Cigars	55,879	1,466		22.0 cir
Artificial and preserved flowers	5,657	1,461		No data by states
Knitted outerwear, contract factories	2,715	1,449		0
Underwear, women's and children's, knitted	10,453	1,431		4.0 cir
Linen goods	1,862	1,399		0
Rayon woven goods, 18 inches and over	57,949	1,391	**1,279**	36.0
Silk broad woven goods	17,597	1,376		12.0 cir
Knitted underwear	39,923	1,361	**1,177**	33.3
Worsted yarn	17,303	1,355		1.0 cir
Dresses, house, uniform, etc.	28,250	1,353		1.0 cir
Boxes, cigar	3,296	1,349		26.0 cir
Hosiery	150,460	1,340	**1,109**	44.2
Curtains and draperies, contract factories	711	1,317		0
Cotton goods woven, over 12 inches	336,104	1,313	**1,277**	74.0
Brooms	4,067	1,310	**994**	18.4
Handkerchiefs, regular factories	4,065	1,305		10.0 cir
Men's and boys' shirts (except work), collars, nightwear, regular fact.	55,570	1,298		13.0 cir
Gloves and mittens, leather	11,637	1,289		0
Rayon yarn processed for sale	5,399	1,283		11.0 cir
Dresses, except house, contract factories	43,874	1,273		1.0 cir
Men's and boys' clothing, contract factories	43,953	1,244		0.2 cir
Cotton yarn and thread	86,206	1,224	**1,108**	78.5
Silk yarn and thread (for sale)	10,572	1,205		7.0 cir
Underwear, women's and children's, woven	8,835	1,183		2.0 cir
Gloves and mittens, cloth or cloth and leather	12,679	1,093		9.0 cir
Gloves and mittens, knitted	3,182	1,089		0
Men's and boys' trousers and wash suits	15,817	1,081		25.0 cir
Baskets and willow ware	9,308	1,041		39.0 cir
Men's and boys' work and sport clothing	69,502	1,029	**788**	35.3
Furnishing goods, men's, contract factories	759	1,018		0
Rayon throwing and spinning, commission	1,937	995		0
Clothing, women's and misses' not elsewhere classified, cont. factories	5,178	918		0
Outerwear, children's, contract factories	5,157	905		3.0 cir
Blouses, women's and misses', contract factories	2,554	896		0
Silk throwing and spinning for sale	13,290	876		4.0 cir
Handkerchiefs, contract factories	932	869		0
Men's and boys' underwear, regular factories	7,888	834		18.0 cir
Dresses, house, uniform, etc., contract factories	4,039	734		1.0 cir
Men's and boys' shirts (except work), contract factories	12,024	667		1.0
Men's and boys' underwear, contract factories	1,424	535		0

Bold-faced figures indicate value added per wage earner in the Southeast.

is above average in all except wages, but does not reach as high as cigarette manufacture with which it is usually associated.[20]

SUMMARY OF GROUP I

There are, then, 44 industries (among the 352 into which the *Census of Manufactures* divides the industry of the United States) in which the Southeast has from 20 percent to 100 percent of the wage earners. By indices other than number of wage earners the region may not have so large a share of these industries. Low wages in the Southeast mean that the region has in practically every instance a smaller share of the total wage outlay in a given industry than its proportion of the wage earners. Less skill, less technical application, and more concentration in the cheaper types of products mean that in practically all the 44 industries the Southeast has a smaller proportion of the value of product and of the value

[20] For indices see table at end of chapter.

INDUSTRIES WITH HIGHEST WAGES PER WAGE EARNER
Forty-nine Industries With Wages Per Wage Earner More Than $1,400

Industry	Number of wage earners	Wages per wage earner		Percent wage earners in Southeast
Photoengraving	12,364	2,355	1,928	4.5
Stereotyping and electrotyping	4,766	2,034		*1.0 cir*
Malt	1,644	1,770		0
Models and patterns (not paper)	5,728	1,704		No data by states
Machine tool accessories, precision instruments	32,893	1,701		*0.1 cir*
Petroleum refining	83,182	1,688		*6.0 cir*
Liquors, malt	47,037	1,685	1,360	5.8
Fur goods	12,798	1,670		*0.1 cir*
Machine tools	47,266	1,656		*0.6 cir*
Locomotives	9,000	1,649		No data by states
Blast-furnace products	23,075	1,647		*10.0 cir*
Newspapers and periodicals	135,215	1,641	1,351	8.9
Printers' machinery and equipment	13,716	1,632		*1.0 cir*
Steel works and rolling mill products	479,342	1,627		*4.0 cir*
Motor vehicles	194,527	1,625		*2.0 cir*
Coke oven products	20,603	1,607		*11.0 cir*
Explosives	5,406	1,595		*1.0 cir*
Cash registers and calculating machines	23,630	1,584		*0.1 cir*
Baking powder, yeast, etc	2,380	1,580		*3.0 cir*
Agricultural implements including tractors	77,512	1,572		*2.0 cir*
Photographic materials	18,450	1,565		*0.5 cir*
Engines, turbines, water wheels, etc	32,855	1,547		*0.3 cir*
Motor vehicle bodies and parts	284,814	1,545		*1.0 cir*
Soda fountain and related products	1,655	1,541		No data by states
Rubber tires and tubes	63,290	1,528		*1.0 cir*
Forgings not made in rolling mills	18,255	1,515		*1.0 cir*
Ship and boat building	62,274	1,505		*18.0 cir*
Sewing machines	9,019	1,502		0
Cranes, dredging and road building machinery	18,800	1,497		*0.5 cir*
Lithographing	24,079	1,492		*2.0 cir*
Corn sirups, etc., and starch	7,010	1,490		0
Smelting and refining zinc	11,265	1,488		?
Steel springs (except wire) not made in rolling mills	3,902	1,487		0
Chemicals not elsewhere classified (some 200)	78,951	1,485	1,176	9.7
Machinery not elsewhere classified (over 100 kinds)	146,712	1,484	1,074	4.1
Abrasives	9,670	1,474		*1.0 cir*
Cars, electric and steam	40,466	1,465		*4.0 cir*
Ink, printing	2,793	1,463		*1.5 cir*
Asphalted-felt-base floor covering	3,280	1,455		0
Smelting and refining copper	14,514	1,443		*2.0 cir*
Coats and suits, women's and misses'	20,690	1,436		*0.5 cir*
Machine shop products	109,245	1,422	1,145	3.3
Compressed and liquefied gases	4,655	1,416		*7.0 cir*
Doors, sashes, etc. (iron and steel)	8,408	1,413		*3.0 cir*
Firearms	6,847	1,412		0
Lapidary work	217	1,411		0
Tin foil, etc	1,669	1,410		No data by states
Refrigerators, etc	50,623	1,410		*2.0 cir*
Pumps, etc., air compressors	28,320	1,404		*0.5 cir*

Bold-faced figures indicate wages per wage earner in the Southeast.

added by manufacture than its percent of the wage earners indicate. This problem will be discussed further in Chapter V.

Since the region has 21.5 percent of the population it may be said that in these 44 industries it manufactures more than it uses—manufactures for the national market. Within the limitations of this measure noted in Chapter I, these 44 industries belong, by definition, to Group I. They also belong to Group I—and to the region—by nature. All of these industries except one are based directly or indirectly on a natural or agricultural resource of the region, many of which are peculiar to the region. This one, distilled liquors, probably depends largely upon grains raised outside the region. Located mostly in Kentucky, it belongs there by virtue of historic skills and reputation.

For better or for worse these belong in the Southeast, and are important to its agricultural and industrial economy. It is the misfortune—in some

MANUFACTURING FOR THE NATION

Industries With Highest Value Added by Manufacture Per Wage Earner

Fifty-one Industries With Value Added of More Than $5,000

Industry	Number of wage earners	Value added by manufacture per wage earner		Percent of wage earners in Southeast
Flavoring extracts and sirups	4,162	$17,200		12.0 cir
Chewing gum	2,401	16,600		2.0 cir
Bluing	67	11,614		2.0 cir
Malt	1,644	11,250		0
Oleomargarine not made in meat-packing establishments	1,214	11,160		0
Drugs and medicines	24,095	10,255	8,303	5.5
Cleaning and polishing preparations	3,341	10,245		1.0 cir
Liquors, rectified and blended	7,094	10,160	9,736	4.1
Compressed and liquefied gases	4,655	9,060		7.0
Insecticides, etc.	4,322	8,576		10.0 cir
Cereal preparations	8,133	8,560		2.0 cir
Lubricating oils not made in petroleum refineries	2,231	8,393		2.0 cir
Soap	14,008	8,290		2.0 cir
Foundry supplies	466	8,340		No data by states
Ink, printing	2,793	7,964		1.5 cir
Perfumes, cosmetics, etc.	10,158	7,721		3.0 cir
Cigarettes	26,149	7,549	7,696	94.7
Newspapers and periodicals	135,215	7,418	5,707	8.9
Ice cream	18,664	7,416	5,273	12.8
Blackings, stains and dressings	1,536	7,288		6.0 cir
Shortenings, cooking and salad oils	4,901	7,160		15.0 cir
Paints, pigments and varnish	31,664	7,149	6,198	4.1
Malt liquors	47,037	7,126	4,967	5.8
Baking powder, yeast, etc.	2,380	7,122		3.0 cir
Billiard and pool tables, bowling alleys, etc.	530	6,998		2.0 cir
Mucilage, etc.	295	6,931		0
Distilled liquors	6,215	6,420	6,026	34.1
Vinous liquors	3,005	6,370		2.0 cir
Gold, silver and platinum refining (not from ore)	1,085	6,346		0
Explosives	5,406	6,284		1.0 cir
Graphite, ground and refined	56	6,231		0
Chemicals not elsewhere classified	78,951	6,050	6,463	9.7
Linseed oil and cake	2,628	6,041		0
Beverages, nonalcoholic	27,979	5,876	6,149	30.4
Manufactured ice	18,705	5,829	4,965	26.4
Petroleum refining	83,182	5,800		6.0 cir
Corn sirup, etc., and starch	7,010	5,610		0
Blast-furnace products	23,075	5,532		10.0 cir
Paving materials—blocks, etc.	1,946	5,490		No data by states
Stereotyping and electrotyping	4,766	5,432		1.0 cir
Oils not elsewhere classified	2,474	5,402		10.0 cir
Ink, writing	366	5,398		0
Roofing, asphalt shingles, etc.	7,418	5,381		3.0 cir
Oils, essentials	195	5,373		7.0 cir
Carbon paper and inked ribbons	1,627	5,336		0
Feeds, prepared for animals and fowls	14,397	5,328	3,904	12.5
Bone black, carbon black, etc.	2,190	5,305		19.3
Fire extinguishers (chemical)	1,041	5,098		0
Photoengraving	12,364	5,068	4,397	4.5
Flour and other grain mill products	26,390	5,063	3,358	14.5
Abrasives	9,670	5,027		1.0 cir

Bold-faced figures indicate value added per wage earner in the Southeast.

cases the fault—of the Southeast that by and large they are low wage, low value-creating industries. Seventeen of the 44 are among the 50 odd industries at the lowest wage scale in the nation, *i.e.*, those paying less than $800 per wage earner. Thirteen more pay less than $800 in that portion of the industry located in the Southeast. Not one rises to the list of high wage industries of the nation; only three pay more than the average for all industries in the United States. Of the portion in the Southeast only two have a wage per wage earner of over a thousand dollars. Twelve of the 44 are among the lowest 40 odd industries in the nation in value added per wage earner, *i.e.*, those producing less than $1,600 per wage earner. Seven more produce less than $1,600 per wage earner in the

MANUFACTURING FOR THE NATION—

Industries	Percent wage earners in Southeast*	Number of wage earners U.S.	Number of wage earners S.E.	Wages per wage earner U.S.	Wages per wage earner S.E.	Value of product per wage earner U.S.	Value of product per wage earner S.E.	Value added by mfr. per wage earner U.S.	Value added by mfr. per wage earner S.E.
Cane sugar manufacture	100.0	4,221	4,221	565	565	6,920	6,920	1,995	1,995
Turpentine and rosin	100.0	1,506	1,506	232	232	19,273	19,273	4,220	4,220
Cigarettes	94.7	26,149	24,762	925	922	17,500†	17,358†	7,549	7,696
Cotton yarn and thread	78.5	86,206	67,674	659	610	3,023	2,862	1,224	1,108
Cotton woven goods	74.0	336,104	248,800	761	729	2,877	2,881	1,313	1,277
Cottonseed oil, meal, cake	68.0	16,583	11,259	514	495	14,596	14,765	2,792	2,522
Wood distillation	68 cir	4,467	884M	901	902M	5,853	7,450M	3,317	4,840M
Rice cleaning and polishing	67.0	2,218	1,486	611	474	21,124	17,579	3,623	2,565
Fertilizers	62.3	20,893	13,017	735	539	9,370	8,608	3,144	2,660
Cast iron pipe	60 cir	17,613	8,316A	1,027	916A	3,470	3,380A	2,026	2,003A
Tobacco, chewing and snuff	48 cir	10,130	no data	848	no data	9,590†	no data	4,517	no data
Rayon and allied products	45 cir	55,098	10,637V	1,185	1,220V	4,623	5,252V	3,159	3,600V
Lumber and timber products	44.5	323,928	144,124	849	532	2,619	1,955	1,555	1,120
Hosiery	44.2	150,460	66,458	906	714	2,403	2,137	1,340	1,109
Tanning materials, etc.	40 cir	2,812	412NC	1,067	868NC	12,690	8,240NC	4,652	3,420NC
Wooden boxes (except cigars)	39.6	25,981	10,298	752	498	3,323	2,124	1,574	1,058
Baskets and willow ware, etc.	39 cir	9,308	1,057V	551	313V	1,789	1,053V	1,041	600V
Rayon woven goods (broad)	36.0	57,949	20,865	845	794	3,965	3,806	1,391	1,279
Men's work clothing, etc.	35.3	69,502	24,577	594	481	2,941	2,604	1,029	788
Cooperage	35 cir	9,588	1,071K	957	775K	5,238	4,920K	1,846	1,810
Dyeing and finishing yarn	35 cir	7,344	1,006T	944	900T	2,943	2,214T	2,015	1,661T
Distilled liquors	34.1	6,215	2,122	1,193	979	18,198	19,196	6,420	6,026
Dyeing and finishing cotton fabrics	34 cir	49,635	7,189NC	987	760NC	4,111	7,070NC	1,972	2,660NC
Wood preserving	34 cir	12,401	1,096M	914	650	9,410	6,615M	2,582	1,890M
Knitted underwear	33.3	39,923	13,276	715	647	2,950	2,650	1,361	1,177
Cordage and twine	33 cir	14,043	1,653G	832	603G	4,730	2,878G	2,022	904G
Beverages, nonalcoholic	30.4	27,979	8,466	1,107	963	9,892	10,540	5,876	6,149
Bags, other than paper	30 cir	12,075	971L	807	677L	10,766	13,780L	2,176	2,460L
Planing mill products	28.2	66,814	18,810	1,014	702	4,678	3,850	2,062	1,516
Wood, turned and shaped, etc.	27.4	23,087	6,337	844	707	3,044	2,688	1,621	1,300
Cane sugar refining	27 cir	14,024	3,181L	1,140	700L	30,200	23,630L	4,410	3,560L
Manufactured ice	26.4	18,705	4,945	1,155	870	7,300	6,306	5,829	4,965
Canned and cured fish, etc.	26.0	18,229	4,704	478	284	4,301	2,160	1,628	905
Bags, paper	26 cir	10,360	1,044L	951	816L	7,959	8,060L	2,803	2,110L
Boxes, cigar, wooden	26 cir	3,296	711F	704	585F	2,163	1,844F	1,349	1,335F
Pulp	25 cir	26,994	1,823V	1,244	1,090V	9,157	9,950V	3,465	3,160V
Men's trousers, suits, etc. (wash)	25 cir	15,817	1,598G	603	436G	2,957	2,471G	1,081	584G
Minerals, earth, ground	25 cir	4,539	384G	1,079	836G	4,662	5,540G	3,425	3,140G
Lime	24 cir	9,751	1,072V	986	682V	3,592	2,327V	2,229	1,280V
Excelsior	23 cir	960	160V	760	550V	3,160	2,387V	1,769	1,000V
Furniture (household and office)	22.7	170,072	38,538	1,015	758	3,870	3,080	2,060	1,505
Marble, cut and shaped	22.5	20,816	4,692	1,171	876	3,795	2,753	2,482	1,930
Cigars	22 cir	55,879	9,966F	671	690F	2,799†	2,270F†	1,466	1,238F
Curtains and draperies, etc.	20 cir	8,934	1,253G	661	530G	5,878	4,920G	1,709	1,840G

*Share of the Southeast usually considerably lower by other indices. See Chapter V.   †Revenue tax deducted.

Key to abbreviations: A, Alabama; F, Florida; G, Georgia; K, Kentucky; L, Louisiana; M, Mississippi; NC, North Carolina; T, Tennessee; V, Virginia. The state with the largest number of wage earners is used as a sample of the Southeast when regional data are unavailable.

The indices for the industries in which the Southeast has from 20-100 percent of the wage earners are recapitulated here for convenience in reference. Columnar arrangement makes it possible to compare any one item of all industries better than can be done with the individual industry tables in the text.

The most striking single fact shown by this table is that these are low index industries wherever they are located. Considering first the United States' column, three-fourths have a wage per wage earner for the whole industry of less than $1,000, and only 3 (rayon, distilled liquors, and pulp) reached the national average of $1,180. Several are high in value of product per wage earner indicating that they are important users of raw materials. But in value added per wage earner 30 of the 44 are below the national average of $2,938. While some are low in salary per salaried person, about half reach the national average of $2,232. They do so chiefly because they employ relatively few salaried persons: 33 of the 44 employ more wage earners per salaried person than the national average (7), and portion of the industry in the Southeast. Nineteen of the 44 appear in both the lowest wage and the lowest value-added lists.

For better or for worse these industries should be in the Southeast. But they are neither profitable enough nor solid enough to depend upon

Group I Industries

Percent wages are of value added by mfr.		Salary per salaried person		Salary per wage earner		Wage earners per salaried person		Wage and salary per wage earner		Percent wages and salary are of value added by mfr.		Balance per wage earner, for interest, profits, taxes, etc.	
U.S.	S.E.	U.S.	S.E.	U.S.	S.E.	U.S.	S.E.	U.S.	S.E.	U.S.	S.E.	U.S.	S.E.
28.3	28.3	1,386	1,386	197	197	7.1	7.1	762	762	38.2	38.2	1,233	1,233
5.5	5.5	664	664	577	577	1.2	1.2	809	809	19.2	19.2	3,411	3,411
12.2	12.0	2,459	2,455	142	138	17.4	17.7	1,067	1,060	14.1	13.8	6,482	6,636
53.8	55.1	2,164	2,155	79	55	27.4	39.1	738	665	60.2	60.1	486	443
58.0	57.0	2,406	2,437	60	52	40.3	46.6	821	781	62.5	61.2	492	496
18.4	19.6	2,028	2,063	341	305	6.0	6.8	855	800	30.6	31.7	1,937	1,722
27.1	18.7M	1,914	2,123M	239	222M	8.0	9.6M	1,140	1,124M	34.4	23.3M	2,177	3,716M
16.9	18.5	2,196	2,010	557	488	3.9	4.1	1,168	962	32.2	37.4	2,455	1,603
23.4	20.3	1,902	1,742	305	271	6.2	6.5	1,040	810	33.1	30.5	2,104	1,850
50.6	45.8A	2,379	2,332A	164	138A	14.5	16.9A	1,191	1,054A	58.8	52.6A	835	949A
18.8	no data	2,339	no data	267	no data	8.8	no data	1,115	no data	24.7	no data	3,402	no data
37.5	33.0V	2,239	2,482V	210	258V	10.6	9.6V	1,395	1,478V	44.2	40.0V	1,764	2,122V
54.6	47.5	2,166	2,043	107	92	20.2	22.1	956	624	61.5	55.7	599	496
67.6	64.5	2,236	2,321	100	78	22.2	29.5	1,006	792	75.2	71.5	334	317
22.9	25.4NC	2,893	2,703NC	859	434NC	3.4	6.2NC	1,926	1,202NC	41.4	35.1NC	2,726	2,218NC
47.8	47.1	2,244	2,304	172	105	13.1	22.0	924	603	58.7	57.0	650	455
52.9	52.2V	2,079	2,060V	127	44V	16.3	46.0V	678	357V	65.1	59.6V	363	243V
60.8	62.1	2,160	1,994	91	57	23.7	35.0	936	851	67.2	66.6	455	428
57.8	61.1	1,808	1,687	94	60	19.2	28.3	688	541	67.0	68.6	341	247
51.9	42.8K	2,435	2,162K	167	69K	14.6	31.6K	1,124	844K	60.9	46.6K	722	966K
46.9	54.1T	2,844	2,360T	316	141T	9.0	16.6T	1,260	1,041	62.5	62.6T	755	620T
18.6	16.2	2,205	2,207	457	477	4.8	4.6	1,650	1,456	25.7	24.2	4,770	4,570
50.0	28.6NC	2,374	1,860NC	253	94NC	9.4	19.8NC	1,240	854NC	62.8	32.1NC	732	1,806NC
35.4	34.4M	2,056	2,240M	157	106M	13.1	21.0M	1,071	756M	41.5	40.0M	1,511	1,134M
52.5	55.0	2,157	2,262	144	94	15.0	24.1	859	741	63.0	63.0	502	436
41.2	66.7G	2,479	2,008G	211	56G	11.8	35.9G	1,043	659G	51.6	73.0G	979	245G
18.8	15.7	2,301	2,646	552	565	4.2	4.6	1,659	1,528	28.3	25.0	4,217	4,621
37.1	27.5L	2,483	2,223L	282	234L	8.8	9.5L	1,089	911L	50.0	37.2L	1,087	1,549L
49.0	46.4	1,988	1,818	296	201	6.7	9.1	1,310	903	63.5	59.6	752	613
52.0	54.4	2,107	2,085	206	153	10.2	13.5	1,050	860	64.8	66.2	571	440
258.	19.7L	2,340	1,814L	283	135L	8.3	13.3L	1,423	835L	32.2	23.4L	2,987	2,725L
19.7	17.5	1,840	1,556	591	568	3.1	2.7	1,746	1,438	30.0	29.0	4,083	3,527
29.4	31.4	2,189	1,600	122	58	18.0	27.5	600	342	36.9	37.9	1,028	562
33.9	38.7L	2,693	1,995L	265	108L	10.2	18.3L	1,216	924L	43.4	43.8L	1,587	1,186L
52.2	43.8F	2,624	3,030F	152	98F	17.2	31.0F	856	683F	63.5	51.1F	493	652F
35.9	34.5V	2,392	2,790V	191	219V	12.5	12.7V	1,435	1,309V	41.4	41.3V	2,030	1,851V
55.7	74.8G	2,022	1,784G	134	58G	15.1	30.8G	737	494G	68.1	84.5G	344	90G
31.5	26.6G	2,477	3,061G	378	414G	6.6	7.4G	1,457	1,250G	42.5	39.8G	1,968	1,890G
44.2	53.3V	2,017	1,825V	160	177V	12.6	10.3V	1,146	859V	51.4	67.1V	1,083	421V
43.0	55.0V	2,102	755V	169	38V	12.5	20.0V	929	588V	52.5	58.8V	840	412V
49.3	50.4	2,149	2,249	243	157	8.8	14.3	1,258	915	61.0	60.5	812	590
47.1	45.4	1,924	1,758	327	232	5.9	7.6	1,498	1,108	60.4	57.4	984	822
45.8	55.7F	1,873	2,018F	102	108F	18.4	18.5F	773	798F	52.7	64.5F	693	440F
38.7	30.4G	2,053	1,831G	253	146G	8.1	12.5G	914	676G	53.5	36.7G	795	1,164G

often the number is two or three times that average. Only 8 expend as much as the national average ($317) on salary per wage earner, and in many cases the amount is so low as to cover only the barest essentials in clerical work and operating supervision. In only 5 of the 44 does the expenditure for salaries and wages per wage earner reach the national average of $1,497. In 27 cases the balance per wage earner for interest, profits, taxes, etc. reaches the national average of $1,441; in 14 cases it is less than half that amount.

If these indices are low for the whole industry it goes without saying that on all scores the showing is even poorer for the part of the industry in the Southeast. Indeed these industries are, by and large, low for the Southeast itself. In 28 of the 44 cases the Southeast wage is lower than the regional average for all industries ($759); in 24 cases the value added by manufacture is lower than the regional average of $1,987. In salary per salaried person about half these industries measure up to the regional average ($2,030) but again this is because there are so few salaried workers: 26 of these industries have more wage earners per salaried person than the regional average of 12.5, and 35 have more than the national average of 7. While they are suited to the Southeast in its present state of technical skill, they offer little opportunity for graduates of technical schools. They also offer little opportunity for clerical and office workers.

for industrial balance. Many are stationary or declining industries. The region needs to build up the further processing of some semifinished products of these 44. It needs to practice selectivity in regard to expansion of the 44—ceasing to seek or even to welcome some of them. More than this, it needs to look for and encourage industries of the types in Group II and Group III.

CHAPTER III

MANUFACTURING FOR THE REGION—
GROUP II INDUSTRIES

The Southeast has had some experience in developing and operating a number of industries besides those in which it manufactures for the nation. Enough experience to show that the region can raise the needed capital, provide or procure the technical skill, train the labor for the semiskilled jobs and find a market for the product. Some of these industries are based as directly on natural resources and crops as those described in Chapter II of which the region has from 20 percent to 100 percent of the wage earners. Others are based on the semimanufactured products of its larger industries. It would seem possible, therefore, that in some of those branches of manufacturing the region could expand to meet its proportionate demand for the products and in others it might expand sufficiently to manufacture for the nation. It would seem logical that in this category of industries there are to be found some which planning groups should emphasize and chambers of commerce could afford to encourage. Among them are a number of industries an increase of which would aid in the optimum development of the region. They would give variety to the economic base. Some would furnish a market for products of agriculture and extractive industries. Most important, many are high index industries, paying wages and creating values per wage earner higher than the national and regional averages. There are 39 of this category of industries. In them the Southeast has from 4 to 19.3 percent of the wage earners. Inasmuch as the emphasis here is on the presence of some experience and skills instead of the region's share in the national industry, as in Chapter II, it seemed useful to discuss them by large industry groups rather than in the order of percentages in the region.

FOOD PRODUCTS INDUSTRIES

Bread and Other Bakery Products. The indices show that some of the industries in the food products group are far more promising than others. An average one is bread and bakery products. The statistics for this industry are as follows:

MANUFACTURING FOR THE REGION

Bread and other bakery products	United States	South-east	Percent
Number of wage earners	239,388	22,116	9.2
Wage per wage earner	$ 1,225	$ 955	78.0
Value of product per wage earner	$ 5,975	$ 5,300	88.7
Value added by manufacture per wage earner	$ 2,922	$ 2,530	86.6
Percent wages are of value added by manufacture	42.0	37.9	
Salary per salaried person	$ 1,914	$ 1,713	89.5
Salary per wage earner	$ 190	$ 182	95.8
Number of wage earners per salaried person	10.1	9.5	94.0
Wage and salary per wage earner	$ 1,415	$ 1,137	80.4
Percent wage and salary are of value added by manufacture	48.4	44.9	
Balance for interest, profits, taxes	$ 1,507	$ 1,393	92.4

The region's wage per wage earner, though considerably lower than for the whole industry, is well above the average for all industries in the Southeast ($759). The value added by manufacture compares even more favorably with the regional average for all industries ($1,987). The balance left for interest, etc. is ample for an industry requiring only moderate investment, the average capital assets per wage earner of 9 large companies being $3,400. Bread is, in the main, produced locally for local markets. In the Southeast its market is so limited by the southern preference for and the cheapness of home-cooked hot breads that the 9.2 percent of the industry (based on wage earners) probably supplies a far larger proportion of the region's bread than this percentage would indicate. These habits are changing, however, as is shown by the fact that the number of wage earners in bakeries has been increasing rapidly between 1929 and 1937. For example, wage earners increased 69.6 percent in North Carolina, 46.2 percent in Florida and 39.5 percent in Georgia between those years. The whole industry is growing. The total number of wage earners increased 49.2 percent between 1925 and 1937. The Southeast might well develop this industry further, and especially in the field of cake, cookie and cracker manufacture of which the Southeast has little. With 14.5 percent of the wage earners in the flour mill industry and about 27 percent in cane sugar refining, it can be seen that the region possesses the main raw materials for expanding the industry.

Ice Cream. The case of ice cream is very similar. With 12.8 percent of the wage earners the Southeast may now be making as much ice cream as possible considering its milk supply, and as much as its population can

Ice cream	United States	South-east	Percent
Number of wage earners	18,664	2,391	12.8
Wage per wage earner	$ 1,140	$ 892	78.2
Value of product per wage earner	$15,109	$11,193	74.1
Value added by manufacture per wage earner	$ 7,416	$ 5,273	71.1
Percent wages are of value added by manufacture	15.4	16.9	
Salary per salaried person	$ 1,911	$ 1,839	96.2
Salary per wage earner	$ 597	$ 697	116.8
Number of wage earners per salaried person	3.2	2.6	81.2
Wage and salary per wage earner	$ 1,737	$ 1,589	91.5
Percent wage and salary are of value added by manufacture	23.4	30.2	
Balance for interest, profits, taxes	$ 5,679	$ 3,684	64.9

afford to buy. The industry's greater importance, as will be shown in Group III (Chapter IV), will come in developing a market for a potential farm product. It is one of the high index industries by most measures and the portion located in the Southeast is well above the regional average on all counts. Between 1925 and 1937 the industry increased 78 percent in value of product and 50 percent in value added by manufacture.

Prepared Animal Feeds. A similar situation is found in the prepared animal feed industry. With its present inattention to poultry and animal raising the Southeast's 12.5 percent of the wage earners may be sufficient to supply its market, though every farmer and frequenter of supply stores is aware of the large amount of "ship stuff" that comes from other regions. With the encouragement of other industries such as poultry dressing, meat packing, and egg using industries to furnish markets for animal products, the Southeast would need an increasing amount of prepared feed, just as encouragement of milling and meat packing would supply raw material in the form of by-products. This industry is undoubtedly growing, its total number of wage earners having increased 70.4 percent between 1931 and 1937. The industry as a whole has a good wage index and, though the part in the Southeast averages only $708 per wage earner, this figure is well above the wage in several of the large industries employing a high proportion of Negro male labor as, for example, cotton seed oil ($495), fertilizer ($539), lumber and timber ($532). In value added by manufacture per wage earner even in the Southeast the industry is well above the national average—high enough, in fact, to warrant higher wages if the labor supply made it necessary to pay more.

FEEDS, PREPARED (ANIMAL)	United States	Southeast	Percent
Number of wage earners	14,397	1,804	12.5
Wage per wage earner	$ 1,100	$ 708	64.4
Value of product per wage earner	$28,840	$19,982	69.3
Value added by maufacture per wage earner	$ 5,328	$ 3,904	73.3
Percent wages are of value added by manufacture	20.6	18.2	
Salary per salaried person	$ 1,804	$ 1,744	96.7
Salary per wage earner	$ 600	$ 613	102.2
Number of wage earners per salaried person	3.0	2.8	93.3
Wage and salary per wage earner	$ 1,700	$ 1,321	77.7
Percent wage and salary are of value added by manufacture	32.0	33.8	
Balance for interest, profits, taxes	$ 3,628	$ 2,583	71.2

Canned Fruits and Vegetables. Two other industries of the food group in which the Southeast has had considerable experience are canned fruits and vegetables, etc., and food not elsewhere classified. The first of these is a great employer of labor, though on a highly seasonal basis. It is growing rapidly, having increased 59.6 percent in number of wage earners between 1925 and 1937. It is growing even more rapidly in certain southeastern states; for example, Virginia and Florida have more than doubled their wage earners since 1929. The region now has 11.3 percent of all the wage earners in the industry. The wage per wage earner in the Southeast is only $357, one of the lowest in the region. The value added by manufacture is low partly because the Southeast cans the cheaper products, which, after deduction of salaries and wages, leaves a balance of only $622. This holds little promise of much better wages, since it is probably only the low wage and low capital investment which now keeps the industry going. The industry as a whole shows indices roughly twice as high as those for the Southeast, but even then its wage of $676 puts it in the lowest 10 percent of all industries in the United States, and it is by far the largest industry that falls so low. The chief value of this industry to the Southeast is that it furnishes a market for more varied farm products.

CANNED FRUITS, VEGETABLES, ETC.	United States	Southeast	Percent
Number of wage earners	137,164	15,496	11.3
Wage per wage earner	$ 676	$ 357	52.8
Value of product per wage earner	$ 5,756	$ 2,901	50.4
Value added by manufacture per wage earner	$ 2,118	$ 1,054	49.8
Percent wages are of value added by manufacture	31.9	33.9	
Salary per salaried person	$ 1,840	$ 1,395	75.8
Salary per wage earner	$ 146	$ 75	51.4
Number of wage earners per salaried person	12.6	18.6	147.6
Wage and salary per wage earner	$ 822	$ 432	52.6
Percent wage and salary are of value added by manufacture	38.9	41.0	
Balance for interest, profits, taxes	$ 1,296	$ 622	48.0

Miscellaneous Prepared Foods. Miscellaneous food preparations is a composite industry made up of meat products, peanut butter, mixed sirup, blended cheeses, potato chips, ice cream cones, malted milk, etc. The Southeast has the raw materials for several of the important items in the list, while others would increase with the encouragement of materials for industries in Group II. With the South's pride in and reputation for good foods, the exploitation of its characteristic recipes might well form the basis for developing branches of this industry. The industry shows more promise as a user of raw materials than it does as a purveyor of good wages. The value added by manufacture and balance after wages and salaries suggests that it might pay higher wages if necessary. The number of wage earners increased 87.9 percent between 1931 and 1937, and these are types of foods that are growing in popularity.

MISCELLANEOUS FOOD PREPARATIONS	United States	Southeast	Percent
Number of wage earners	16,794	1,450	8.6
Wage per wage earner	$ 915	$ 582	63.6
Value of product per wage earner	$16,592	$11,584	69.8
Value added by manufacture per wage earner	$ 4,634	$ 3,084	66.6
Percent wages are of value added by manufacture	19.8	18.8	
Salary per salaried person	$ 2,170	$ 2,122	97.8
Salary per wage earner	$ 453	$ 350	77.3
Number of wage earners per salaried person	4.8	6.1	127.1
Wage and salary per wage earner	$ 1,368	$ 932	68.1
Percent wage and salary are of value added by manufacture	29.5	30.2	
Balance for interest, profits, taxes	$ 3,266	$ 2,152	65.9

Shortenings and Vegetable Oils. In two other industries of the food group, confectionery and shortening and vegetable salad oil, the Southeast already has more than an abundance of materials in the semifinished products of two of its large industries, sugar refining and cottonseed oil industries, respectively. Due to limitations of census data it is impossible to do more than guess what portion of the shortening oil industry is in the Southeast: the rough estimate of 15 percent may be considerably short of the mark. Although this industry employs a small number of workers its high indices make it so desirable that the Southeast would do well to encourage it up to the 68 percent which the region has of the cottonseed oil industry. It increased 34 percent in the number of wage earners and doubled in value added by manufacture between 1933 and 1937. Some of this apparent growth may be recovery from depression lows, but certainly not all, considering the growing popularity of these oils for dressings and cooking. Expansion in this industry also brings growth in tin can and paper box making.

SHORTENINGS (EXCEPT LARD), SALAD OILS	United States	Tennessee*	Percent
Number of wage earners	4,901	726	
Wage per wage earner	$ 1,150	$ 872	75.8
Value of product per wage earner	$48,862	$50,216	102.8
Value added by manufacture per wage earner	$ 7,160	$ 4,250	59.4
Percent wages are of value added by manufacture	16.1	20.5	
Salary per salaried person	$ 2,030	$ 2,118	104.3
Salary per wage earner	$ 498	$ 365	73.3
Number of wage earners per salaried person	4.1	5.8	141.5
Wage and salary per wage earner	$ 1,648	$ 1,237	75.1
Percent wage and salary are of value added by manufacture	23.0	29.1	
Balance for interest, profits, taxes	$ 5,512	$ 3,013	54.7

*The state with the largest number of employees for which other data are given. Louisiana probably has more wage earners.

Confectionery. The indices for the confectionery industry are low. Planning groups could encourage an increase over the 8.4 percent already located in the Southeast chiefly on the rationalization that it is better than many industries the region already has, especially in value added by manufacture. It is a considerable user of other present or potential products of the region such as packing materials, paper, cardboard, etc. It has increased 67 percent in wage earners and 44.4 percent in value of product since 1925. Capital requirements are relatively high, the assets of 10 companies averaging about $4,500 per wage earner.

CONFECTIONERY	United States	Southeast	Percent
Number of wage earners	53,722	4,491	8.4
Wage per wage earner	$ 809	$ 621	76.8
Value of product per wage earner	$ 5,693	$ 5,238	92.0
Value added by manufacture per wage earner	$ 2,291	$ 2,081	90.8
Percent wages are of value added by manufacture	35.2	29.8	
Salary per salaried person	$ 2,106	$ 1,922	91.3
Salary per wage earner	$ 216	$ 241	111.6
Number of wage earners per salaried person	9.8	8.0	81.6
Wage and salary per wage earner	$ 1,025	$ 862	84.1
Percent wage and salary are of value added by manufacture	44.7	41.4	
Balance for interest, profits, taxes	$ 1,266	$ 1,219	88.4

MANUFACTURING FOR THE REGION

TEXTILE INDUSTRIES

The Southeast has the materials, both raw and processed, for a long list of industries based on cotton and cotton cloth. As has been seen in Chapter II, the textiles as a whole are low index industries. In the cotton cutting-up branches, wages, value added by manufactures and balance for interest, etc. are so low that planners might well leave expansion in this group to the business acumen of entrepreneurs looking for low labor costs.

Men's Shirts. With an estimated 13 percent of the wage earners in men's shirts (except work), the region has had considerable experience in this particular branch, in addition to its 35 percent of the wage earners in the larger work clothing industry discussed in Chapter II. But the indices for the nation are low in this industry and distressingly low in specific states in the Southeast (regional figures unavailable). Cities and towns in the region which have been offering inducements to shirt factories might well ponder the following figures.

MEN'S SHIRTS (EXCEPT WORK)	United States	South Carolina	Percent
Number of wage earners	55,570	1,226	
Wage per wage earner	$ 629	$ 444	70.6
Value of product per wage earner	$ 3,149	$ 1,854	58.9
Value added by manufacture per wage earner	$ 1,298	$ 755	58.2
Percent wages are of value added by manufacture	48.4	68.8	
Salary per salaried person	$ 1,800	$ 1,296	72.0
Salary per wage earner	$ 103	$ 71	68.9
Number of wage earners per salaried person	17.4	18.3	105.2
Wage and salary per wage earner	$ 732	$ 515	70.4
Percent wage and salary are of value added by manufacture	56.4	68.2	
Balance for interest, profits, taxes	$ 566	$ 240	42.4

Awnings, Tents and Sails. One cotton cutting-up industry which has relatively high indices is awnings, tents, sails, etc. The region has had some experience in this, having 8 percent of the wage earners. Its part of the industry compares more favorably with the whole than is the case in any other of the cutting-up group. The region's mills produce types of cloth necessary for these products. Comparable figures earlier than 1935 are unavailable, but even in those two years it increased 18.7 percent in number of wage earners. Defense needs bid fair to cause

AWNINGS, TENTS, SAILS, ETC.	United States	Southeast	Percent
Number of wage earners	4,732	378	8.0
Wage per wage earner	$ 1,024	$ 961	93.8
Value of product per wage earner	$ 6,408	$ 5,565	86.8
Value added by manufacture per wage earner	$ 2,709	$ 2,626	96.9
Percent wages are of value added by manufacture	37.8	36.6	
Salary per salaried person	$ 2,081	$ 2,034	97.7
Salary per wage earner	$ 586	$ 640	109.2
Number of wage earners per salaried person	3.5	3.2	91.4
Wage and salary per wage earner	$ 1,610	$ 1,601	99.4
Percent wage and salary are of value added by manufacture	59.5	60.8	
Balance for interest, profits, taxes	$ 1,099	$ 1,025	93.4

much growth in this industry and the Southeast is the logical place for much of this expansion.

Batting and Padding. It is a little surprising that the Southeast has only about 16 percent of the wage earners in the batting and padding industry. It has the raw materials in the shape of cotton, cotton linters and waste from textile mills. The region has around 30 percent of the wage earners in the household furniture industry which is a great user of such products. North Carolina, with 16,000 wage earners in furniture, has only 151 wage earners in this accessory industry. As a whole it makes a fair showing in wages and value added by manufacture, though in specific southeastern states it is hardly a promising industry.[1]

FOREST PRODUCTS GROUP

The Southeast has 20 percent or more of the wage earners in 11 of the 20 industries in the forest products group. These have been discussed in Chapter II. Most of the others are small and highly specialized.

Caskets and Coffins. The most obvious for the Southeast to encourage is caskets and coffins. With 13.7 percent of the wage earners in the industry the region has sufficient experience and skill for expansion. Any increase, however, would be chiefly transfer of the industry, since it is growing rather slowly; for though the number of wage earners increased 19.2 percent between 1925 and 1937 the value of products is only 1.9 percent larger. The portion in the Southeast has low indices as compared with the whole industry, and rather low even for the region, so that the chief advantage would be in adding more of a type of industry processing regional resources into products that are in common use.

CASKETS, COFFINS, ETC.	United States	Southeast	Percent
Number of wage earners	13,678	1,875	13.7
Wage per wage earner	$ 1,105	$ 797	72.1
Value of product per wage earner	$ 5,246	$ 3,921	74.7
Value added by manufacture per wage earner	$ 2,788	$ 1,727	61.9
Percent wages are of value added by manufacture	39.7	46.0	
Salary per salaried person	$ 2,414	$ 2,321	96.1
Salary per wage earner	$ 426	$ 330	77.3
Number of wage earners per salaried person	5.7	7.05	124.6
Wage and salary per wage earner	$ 1,531	$ 1,127	73.6
Percent wage and salary are of value added by manufacture	54.9	65.2	
Balance for interest, profits, taxes	$ 1,257	$ 600	47.7

PAPER AND ALLIED PRODUCTS

The invention of new techniques has made it possible for industry to use resinous wood heretofore unsuitable for paper manufacture. This, together with the presence of suitable water and cheap electric power in the Southeast, has resulted in a rapid growth of pulp and paper industries. It is likely that this will continue both for natural economic reasons, and because of the effect of the war upon imports from Europe.

[1] Indices in table at end of chapter.

This should not prevent planning groups from doing everything possible to encourage paper manufacturing at least up to the level set by pulp manufacture. The region now has some 25 percent of the wage earners in the pulp industry but only about 7 percent in paper making. The relatively few technologists necessary can easily be imported to make up the region's deficit in the highest skills. It is a high value industry as a whole and the indices for the chief southeastern state are considerably above those for the entire industry.

Paper	United States	Virginia	Percent
Number of wage earners	110,809	2,423	
Wage per wage earner	$ 1,282	$ 1,141	89.0
Value of product per wage earner	$ 8,645	$12,009	140.0
Value added by manufacture per wage earner	$ 3,524	$ 4,580	130.0
Percent wages are of value added by manufacture	36.3	24.9	
Salary per salaried person	$ 2,714	$ 3,043	112.1
Salary per wage earner	$ 287	$ 329	114.6
Number of wage earners per salaried person	9.4	9.2	97.9
Wage and salary per wage earner	$ 1,569	$ 1,470	93.7
Percent wage and salary are of value added by manufacture	44.5	32.1	
Balance for interest, profits, taxes	$ 1,955	$ 3,110	159.1

The paper box industry is less spectacular but is better than the average of all industries in the Southeast in wages and nearly twice the regional average in value added by manufacture. Inasmuch as this is an accessory industry its expansion waits on the development in the region of industries packaging its products in paper boxes. The Southeast has only about 5 percent of the wage earners in this industry.[2]

PRINTING, PUBLISHING AND ALLIED INDUSTRIES

The book, music and job printing industry combines production for the general market with other types which amount to local, almost custom, manufacture. The 6.2 percent of the wage earners in the Southeast may well be largely of the latter sort. With its growing paper industry the Southeast will increasingly possess the materials for this industry. Even the writing of books by southerners is increasing. This industry, the eleventh in the United States in number of wage earners, is growing, though rather slowly, having increased 4.3 percent between 1925 and 1937.

Book and Job Printing	United States	Southeast	Percent
Number of wage earners	141,368	8,709	6.2
Wage per wage earner	$ 1,380	$ 1,152	83.5
Value of product per wage earner	$ 5,728	$ 4,550	79.4
Value added by manufacture per wage earner	$ 3,722	$ 2,855	76.7
Percent wages are of value added by manufacture	37.2	40.4	
Salary per salaried person	$ 2,293	$ 1,980	86.3
Salary per wage earner	$ 702	$ 533	75.9
Number of wage earners per salaried person	3.3	3.7	112.1
Wage and salary per wage earner	$ 2,082	$ 1,685	80.9
Percent wage and salary are of value added by manufacture	55.9	59.1	
Balance for interest, profits, taxes	$ 1,640	$ 1,170	71.3

[2] Indices in table at end of chapter.

The meager and uncertain sources of information on capital fail even more signally in this industry because it is a composite of so many types of product; apparently considerable capital per wage earner is necessary for book printing. It is a high index industry.

The Southeast has a smaller percentage of the related bookbinding industry, probably about 4 percent. This is growing somewhat more rapidly (21.6 percent in number of wage earners in the United States between 1925 and 1937). Although only about average by most indices and relatively low in the balance left for interest, etc. ($988), it is higher than most industries in the Southeast. It would be valuable in the region as a further processor of the region's textiles. No census data are available for any southern state.[3]

CHEMICAL AND ALLIED PRODUCTS

Of the 31 industries in the chemical group there are five of which the Southeast has from 20 to nearly 70 percent of the wage earners. These have been discussed in Chapter II. Most of these are the lowest index industries in this group. There are seven additional industries of which the region has from four to nearly 20 percent of the wage earners, and, therefore, has developed a fair amount of experience and skills. The Southeast has also the principal resources for these seven as well as for several smaller industries in which the region has had less experience. These are bone black, carbon black and lamp black; chemicals not otherwise classified; compressed and liquefied gas; drugs and medicine; insecticides; oils not elsewhere classified; and paints, pigments and varnishes.

Bone Black, Carbon Black. The Southeast has 19.3 percent of the wage earners in the small bone black, etc. industry. In view of the fact that the region has few or none of the industries making use of these products directly and few of those using them after further processing, it is likely that the Southeast is already manufacturing these products for the nation. But with the raw materials—coal, wood, tar, petroleum, rosin—it might encourage further expansion, especially since it is a high index industry. Even for the part in the Southeast the per wage earner figures run as follows: wages, $1,058; value added by manufacture, $3,532; balance for interest, etc., $2,339; percent of value added spent on salary and wage, 33.8.

Chemicals, Not Elsewhere Classified. The most promising industry in the group is chemicals not elsewhere classified. This is a large composite of some 150 different chemicals. The Southeast has plants making 55 of these products and has 9.7 percent of the wage earners in the industry. It is growing rapidly, having increased 36.4 percent in wage earners from 1925 to 1937; in value of product, 63.5 percent; and in value added by

[3] Indices in table at end of chapter.

manufacture, 66.2 percent. It is one of the high wage industries of the country, and, though for the part in the Southeast the wage is less than for the whole industry, it is one of the highest in the region. By several measures the Southeast shows up better than the industry as a whole. Capital assets per wage earner for a dozen companies show an extremely wide variation—from $5,000 to $25,000—but the large balance for interest, etc. of nearly $5,000 is sufficient even for the higher range. With 6.2 wage earners per salaried person, it offers many employment opportunities for technically trained persons.

Chemicals, not elsewhere classified	United States	Southeast	Percent
Number of wage earners	78,951	7,626	9.7
Wage per wage earner	$ 1,485	$ 1,176	79.2
Value of product per wage earner	$11,814	$11,900	100.7
Value added by manufacture per wage earner	$ 6,050	$ 6,463	106.8
Percent wages are of value added by manufacture	24.5	18.2	
Salary per salaried person	$ 2,584	$ 2,295	88.8
Salary per wage earner	$ 552	$ 371	67.2
Number of wage earners per salaried person	4.7	6.2	131.9
Wage and salary per wage earner	$ 2,037	$ 1,547	75.9
Percent wage and salary are of value added by manufacture	33.7	23.9	
Balance for interest, profits, taxes	$ 4,013	$ 4,916	125.6

As in the case of pulp and paper, it is likely that the natural advantages of the region will serve to promote the growth of this industry. This, however, is no reason for not extending aid and encouragement for further expansion.

Paints, Pigments and Varnishes. Paints, pigments, and varnishes is the next largest industry in this group of seven. The South has long cited its wealth of minerals and mineral earths some of which are sources of pigments. An expansion of this industry would stimulate the exploitation of these resources. Despite the competition of synthetic resins and petroleum derivative thinners, the industry uses large quantities of turpentine, a southern monopoly product. It uses linseed oil, the production of which would give the region another high index industry and another farm crop. It is particularly important that the paint and varnish industry should be built up now in order that the Southeast may process its much vaunted tung oil. Otherwise the region will repeat the history of its cotton and cottonseed oil industries—send it to other regions for the most profitable process in its production. At present the Southeast has 4.7 percent of the wage earners in the industry. With its present and potential resources it should count on having 40 or 50 percent. The industry increased 24 percent in wage earners and 28 percent in value added by manufacture between 1925 and 1937, a remarkable record in view of the fact that most industries related to building have declined. Capital investment is apparently fairly high, the average of seven companies being about $6,500 per wage earner, but the balance for interest is high also.

The region would be obliged to import technical skills for a while, though its development would offer opportunity for graduates of technical schools.

PAINTS, PIGMENTS, VARNISH	United States	Southeast	Percent
Number of wage earners	31,664	1,498	4.7
Wage per wage earner	$ 1,350	$ 1,050	77.8
Value of product per wage earner	$17,005	$14,455	85.0
Value added by manufacture per wage earner	$ 7,149	$ 6,198	86.7
Percent wages are of value added by manufacture	18.9	17.0	
Salary per salaried person	$ 2,378	$ 2,670	112.3
Salary per wage earner	$ 901	$ 1,090	121.0
Number of wage earners per salaried person	2.6	2.4	92.3
Wage and salary per wage earner	$ 2,251	$ 2,140	95.1
Percent wage and salary are of value added by manufacture	31.5	34.6	
Balance for interest, profits, taxes	$ 4,898	$ 4,058	82.8

Drugs and Medicines. The production of drugs and medicines constitutes another sizeable industry. Its wage index is low but this is apparently an unnecessary state of affairs, for the value added by manufacture is among the highest in the nation. Capital costs are fairly high, the book value of assets of a dozen companies averaging about $7,000 per wage earner. But the balance for interest, etc. is exceeded in only six industries, all much smaller than this: flavoring extracts, chewing gum, bluing, oleomargarine, liquors, rectified and blended, and malt. With its large proportion of technical and clerical workers it offers opportunities for white collar workers. The industry is growing moderately, having increased 14.6 percent in wage earners, 10 percent in value of product and 6.9 percent in value added by manufacture between 1931 and 1937. The Southeast has 5.5 percent of the wage earners. Like all industries manufacturing for the ultimate consumer, increase in this industry would mean an increase in accessory manufacturing such as bottles, boxes and other packaging materials, and printing.

DRUGS AND MEDICINES	United States	Southeast	Percent
Number of wage earners	24,095	1,333	5.5
Wage per wage earner	$ 1,084	$ 732	67.5
Value of product per wage earner	$14,356	$12,482	86.9
Value added by manufacture per wage earner	$10,255	$ 8,303	81.0
Percent wages are of value added by manufacture	10.5	8.8	
Salary per salaried person	$ 2,324	$ 2,002	86.1
Salary per wage earner	$ 949	$ 1,055	111.2
Number of wage earners per salaried person	2.4	1.9	79.2
Wage and salary per wage earner	$ 2,033	$ 1,787	87.9
Percent wage and salary are of value added by manufacture	19.8	21.5	
Balance for interest, profits, taxes	$ 8,222	$ 6,516	79.2

Miscellaneous Chemicals. Of the three smaller industries in the chemical group only a few words are necessary. Compressed and liquid gases, of which the Southeast has about 7 percent of the wage earners, is a very high index industry.[4] Figures on growth are unavailable earlier than 1933; since then the number of wage earners has increased 68.5 percent and the

---
[4] Indices in table at end of chapter.

value of product 76.3 percent and value added 80 percent. It bids fair to continue as it includes the manufacture of "dry ice" and other refrigerants. In insecticides all indices are high except wages. In Florida, which has a few more wage earners than any other southeastern state, wages are very low ($567 per wage earner) but by other measures it is better than the regional average for all industries.[5] Oils not elsewhere classified includes a group of animal oils (fish, lard, and neat's foot oil) and vegetable oils (castor, palm, and soybean). The list includes possibilities for the Southeast to expand beyond its present 10 percent of the wage earners. The indices for individual southeastern states indicate, however, that it is an average, rather than a high, index industry.[6] Its greater importance would be as a market for farm products.

PRODUCTS OF PETROLEUM AND COAL

The only industry to be considered in this group, coke oven products, is of concern chiefly to Alabama. The Southeast has about 11 percent of the wage earners, of whom most are in that state. Other states might encourage their manufacture as by-products of their manufactured gas.[7]

LEATHER AND ITS MANUFACTURES

The Southeast has 5.6 percent of the wage earners in meat packing and roughly 5 percent of those in leather manufacture. Further development of the leather industries awaits the production of the raw materials. There is, however, one industry in this group for which the Southeast has the materials, namely, trunks, suitcases and bags. The statistics of production show that this is a leather industry chiefly by courtesy. If brief cases, the majority of which are still made of leather, are omitted, the nonleather articles outnumber the leather two and one-half to one, and the total value is one and one-half times as great. The Southeast has the wood for framing and the textiles for covering, either plain or made into artificial leather. In 1937 it had only five establishments in this industry and no other regional data are available.[8]

STONE, CLAY AND GLASS PRODUCTS

Clay Products. The Southeast has 18.9 percent of the wage earners in the clay products industry. The chief items are brick and tile and are made in the main for local or semilocal markets. Since the region builds largely of wood it is likely that this percentage of the industry supplies its needs. Like most industries supplying the building trades it has experienced severe decreases since 1925. This is a low index industry.

[5] Indices in table at end of chapter. [6] *Ibid.*
[7] *Ibid.* [8] *Ibid.*

Clay products	United States	South-east	Per-cent
Number of wage earners	59,585	11,237	18.9
Wage per wage earner	$ 971	$ 686	70.6
Value of product per wage earner	$ 2,740	$ 2,162	78.9
Value added by manufacture per wage earner	$ 1,884	$ 1,407	74.7
Percent wages are of value added by manufacture	51.5	48.8	
Salary per salaried person	$ 2,102	$ 2,272	108.1
Salary per wage earner	$ 172	$ 150	87.2
Number of wage earners per salaried person	12.2	15.2	124.6
Wage and salary per wage earner	$ 1,143	$ 836	73.1
Percent wage and salary are of value added by manufacture	60.7	59.4	
Balance for interest, profits, taxes	$ 741	$ 571	77.0

Concrete Products. Concrete products is a parallel industry though with somewhat higher indices. This, too, has suffered decreases since 1925.

Concrete products	United States	South-east	Per-cent
Number of wage earners	12,840	1,735	13.5
Wage per wage earner	$ 1,073	$ 787	73.3
Value of product per wage earner	$ 5,933	$ 4,250	71.6
Value added by manufacture per wage earner	$ 3,171	$ 2,220	70.0
Percent wages are of value added by manufacture	33.9	35.4	
Salary per salaried person	$ 2,046	$ 1,966	96.1
Salary per wage earner	$ 390	$ 342	87.7
Number of wage earners per salaried person	5.2	5.8	111.5
Wage and salary per wage earner	$ 1,463	$ 1,129	77.2
Percent wage and salary are of value added by manufacture	46.1	50.8	
Balance for interest, profits, taxes	$ 1,708	$ 1,091	63.9

Cement. The cement industry is an exception to the general rule that the first processing of a raw material is the lowest index part of the manufacture. The Southeast, with only about four percent of the wage earners in the industry, might well encourage it to supply the region's concrete industry and road building. It requires considerable capital, eight companies for which assets are available ranging from $4,500 to nearly $19,000 invested per wage earner. However the balance for interest, etc. is sufficient to justify such investment.

Cement	United States	Alabama	Per-cent
Number of wage earners	26,426	1,015	
Wage per wage earner	$ 1,289	$ 1,045	81.1
Value of product per wage earner	$ 6,933	$ 7,120	104.1
Value added by manufacture per wage earner	$ 4,284	$ 4,250	99.2
Percent wages are of value added by manufacture	30.1	24.6	
Salary per salaried person	$ 2,467	$ 2,743	111.2
Salary per wage earner	$ 252	$ 265	105.2
Number of wage earners per salaried person	9.8	10.4	106.1
Wage and salary per wage earner	$ 1,541	$ 1,310	85.0
Percent wage and salary are of value added by manufacture	36.0	30.8	
Balance for interest, profits, taxes	$ 2,743	$ 2,940	107.2

Glass. The Southeast needs a larger proportion of the glass industry to supply its own needs for building and to supply its furniture industry. The chief raw material, sand of a suitable quality, is common. While the technical needs are important the professional personnel amounts to less than one percent, so that it would not be difficult to bring sufficient technicians to the region. The skilled workers make up 13.2 percent of the persons attached to the industry. Though this is not much above the average for all manufacturing, it is high for industries in the Southeast. Theirs are specialisms for which experience in other industries is of little use. More than in most manufacturing, the region must literally raise itself by its bootstraps: build a little to train workers to build more of the industry. The Southeast has only about four percent of the wage earners in the glass industry. The industry is growing, having increased 14.0 percent in wage earners, 31 percent in value of product and 35 percent in value added by manufacture between 1925 and 1937.[9]

Wallboard. In the manufacture of products grouped as "wallboard and building insulation, etc." Louisiana, the chief single state, may have enough to place this industry in Group II. Data are not available to show how the indices for this state compare with the industry as a whole. The Southeast has the raw materials for this and the related gypsum products industry. In the latter the region has only a very small beginning. Though small, both are growing industries, and with the increasing interest in insulation and revival in building, bid fair to grow even faster.[10]

IRON AND STEEL PRODUCTS NOT INCLUDING MACHINERY

The organization of the iron and steel industry into a relatively few large companies, some of which operate plants in both the Southeast and other regions, makes it difficult for state or regional encouragement to be effective. The vertical organization of much of the industry, together with the census practice of classifying an establishment according to its chief product, makes it impossible to secure from the census data a satisfactory estimate as to the amount of the specific products manufactured in the Southeast. It appears, however, that of the 28 industries in this group there are 8 of which the Southeast has none and 12 others of which it has very little. One, cast iron pipe, of which it has some 60 percent, has been discussed in Chapter II. The region apparently has some 4 to 10 percent of the remaining 7 categories: blast furnace products, boiler shop products, foundry products, heating and cooking apparatus (not electric), steel barrels and kegs, structural and ornamental steel, and steel works and rolling mill products.

Iron and Steel Industries. All are above average or high wage industries, but not all are high in value added by manufacture considering the great amount of capital invested, estimated at from $8,000 to $10,000 per wage earner. For foundry products and heating and cooking apparatus the regional share can be ascertained with some accuracy. In both cases the wage per wage earner, though above the regional average for all industries, is far below that in the whole industry. The value added by manufacture is low and the sum of wages and salaries per wage earner amounts

[9] Indices in table at end of chapter. [10] *Ibid.*

to well over half the value added, leaving a very small manufacturing margin.[11]

Foundry products	United States	South-east	Per-cent
Number of wage earners	120,024	4,754	4.0
Wage per wage earner	$ 1,321	$ 964	73.0
Value of product per wage earner	$ 3,310	$ 3,082	93.1
Value added by manufacture per wage earner	$ 2,129	$ 1,877	88.2
Percent wages are of value added by manufacture	62.1	51.3	
Salary per salaried person	$ 2,501	$ 2,076	83.0
Salary per wage earner	$ 189	$ 234	123.8
Number of wage earners per salaried person	13.3	8.8	66.2
Wage and salary per wage earner	$ 1,510	$ 1,198	79.3
Percent wage and salary are of value added by manufacture	70.9	63.8	
Balance for interest, profits, taxes	$ 619	$ 679	109.7

Heating and cooking apparatus	United States	South-east	Per-cent
Number of wage earners	89,287	8,642	9.7
Wage per wage earner	$ 1,252	$ 865	69.1
Value of product per wage earner	$ 4,920	$ 2,724	55.4
Value added by manufacture per wage earner	$ 2,903	$ 1,558	53.7
Percent wages are of value added by manufacture	43.1	55.5	
Salary per salaried person	$ 2,127	$ 2,249	105.7
Salary per wage earner	$ 340	$ 153	45.0
Number of wage earners per salaried person	6.3	14.7	233.3
Wage and salary per wage earner	$ 1,592	$ 1,018	63.9
Percent wage and salary are of value added by manufacture	54.8	65.3	
Balance for interest, profits, taxes	$ 1,311	$ 540	41.2

The armament program may cause a great expansion of the iron and steel industries in the Southeast. Even if the specific products needed for defense are made in other regions, it is possible that the Southeast will develop a larger share of the peace time commercial production.

SHIP AND BOAT BUILDING

Like the iron and steel industries, shipbuilding in the Southeast may be greatly increased by the defense program. With its long coast line, many sounds and protected waters suitable for smaller boats, and its fishing industries using large and small craft, the region could well expand this industry. It had, in 1937, about eighteen percent of the wage earners, most of them in Virginia. It is a high wage industry ($1,505 per wage earner), as might be expected, considering the high proportion of skilled workers necessary. The value added by manufacture per wage earner ($2,393) is low in view of the heavy capital investment: wages take 63 percent of the value added by manufacture; wages and salaries together take 75.8 percent, leaving only $579 per wage earner for interest, etc.

MISCELLANEOUS INDUSTRIES

Two industries in the mixed "miscellaneous industries" group for which the Southeast has materials and sufficient experience for expansion are brooms and mattresses and bedsprings. In the first the region has 18.4

[11] Indices for remaining five industries in table at end of chapter.

percent of the wage earners. Considering the fact that many households use homemade brooms it is possible that the region already manufactures as many factory-made brooms as it uses. This is a low index industry all over the United States and so low in the Southeast that its encouragement by public action is hardly justifiable.

Brooms	United States	Southeast	Percent
Number of wage earners	4,067	750	18.4
Wage per wage earner	$ 714	$ 525	73.5
Value of product per wage earner	$ 2,859	$ 2,114	73.9
Value added by manufacture per wage earner	$ 1,310	$ 994	75.9
Percent wages are of value added by manufacture	54.5	52.9	
Salary per salaried person	$ 1,580	$ 1,265	80.1
Salary per wage earner	$ 148	$ 108	73.0
Number of wage earners per salaried person	10.6	11.7	110.4
Wage and salary per wage earner	$ 862	$ 633	73.4
Percent wage and salary are of value added by manufacture	65.8	63.7	
Balance for interest, profits, taxes	$ 448	$ 316	70.5

Some of the indices for the mattress and bedspring industry are low but even for the portion in the Southeast are not as low as in many other cotton and cloth using industries. The region has 14.6 percent of the wage earners. Expansion in this industry would seem to be more promising than in many of the cotton garment industries which are coming to the Southeast.

Mattresses and bedsprings	United States	Southeast	Percent
Number of wage earners	19,165	2,789	14.6
Wage per wage earner	$ 1,034	$ 782	75.6
Value of product per wage earner	$ 5,902	$ 4,884	82.8
Value added by manufacture per wage earner	$ 2,605	$ 2,112	81.1
Percent wages are of value added by manufacture	39.7	37.0	
Salary per salaried person	$ 2,094	$ 2,451	117.0
Salary per wage earner	$ 346	$ 344	99.4
Number of wage earners per salaried person	6.0	7.1	118.3
Wage and salary per wage earner	$ 1,380	$ 1,126	81.6
Percent wage and salary are of value added by manufacture	53.0	53.3	
Balance for interest, profits, taxes	$ 1,225	$ 986	80.5

SUMMARY

There are, then, 39 industries in which the Southeast has the resources, has had some experience, and has developed some skills. Four of these (canned fruits, etc., men's shirts, clay products, and brooms), because of low wage, low value added by manufacture or both, are decidedly unpromising industries. Seven others (confectionery, miscellaneous food preparations, batting and padding, insecticides, foundry products, heating and cooking apparatus, and mattresses and bedsprings) range from doubtful to possible. Some are low wage but high value added or vice versa; others are unpromising only in the part of the industry located in the Southeast. In such cases increase of skills for making the better grade products could easily convert them into desirable industries for the region.

SOUTHERN INDUSTRY

Manufacturing for the Region—

Industries	Percent wage earners in Southeast	Number of wage earners		Wages per wage earner		Value of product per wage earner		Value added by mfr. per wage earner	
		U.S.	S.E.	U.S.	S.E.	U.S.	S.E.	U.S.	S.E.
Bread and other bakery products..	9.2	239,384	22,116	1,225	955	5,975	5,300	2,922	2,530
Canned fruits, vegetables, etc.....	11.3	137,164	15,496	676	357	5,756	2,901	2,118	1,054
Confectionery....................	8.4	53,722	4,491	809	621	5,693	5,238	2,291	2,081
Feeds prepared (animal).........	12.5	14,397	1,804	1,100	708	28,840	19,982	5,328	3,904
Misc. food prep. not elsewh. clsfd..	8.6	16,794	1,450	915	582	16,592	11,584	4,634	3,084
Ice cream.....................	12.8	18,664	2,391	1,140	892	15,109	11,193	7,416	5,273
Shortenings, except lard, salad oils.	15 cir	4,901	726†T	1,150	872T	48,862	50,216T	7,160	4,250T
Batting and padding............	16 cir	4,645	179L	937	362L	7,938	4,818L	2,795	992L
Men's shirts (except work)	13 cir	55,570	1,226SC	629	444SC	3,149	1,854SC	1,298	755SC
Awnings, tents, sails, etc.........	8.0	4,732	378	1,024	961	6,408	5,565	2,709	2,626
Caskets, coffins, etc.............	13.7	13,678	1,875	1,105	797	5,246	3,921	2,788	1,727
Paper.........................	7 cir	110,809	2,423V	1,282	1,141V	8,645	12,009V	3,524	4,580V
Paper boxes...................	5 cir	65,158	705L	1,013	840L	7,205	8,215	2,624	3,420L
Book and job printing...........	6.2	141,368	8,709	1,380	1,152	5,728	4,550	3,722	2,855
Book binding.................	4 cir	25,333	674T	1,132	*	3,743	*	2,529	*
Bone black, carbon black, etc.....	19.3	2,190	422	1,238	1,058	8,609	6,299	5,305	3,532
Chemicals not elsewhere clsfd.....	9.7	78,951	7,626	1,485	1,176	11,814	11,900	6,050	6,463
Compressed and liquefied gases...	7 cir	4,655	117V	1,416	1,175V	12,120	10,320V	9,060	7,625V
Drugs and medicines............	5.5	24,095	1,333	1,084	732	14,356	12,482	10,255	8,303
Insecticides...................	10 cir	4,322	132F	1,078	567F	16,467	7,210F	8,576	2,720F
Oils not elsewhere classified.......	10 cir	2,474	96V	1,197	890V	28,083	10,455V	5,402	2,322V
Paints, pigments, varnish.........	4.7	31,664	1,498	1,350	1,050	17,005	14,455	7,149	6,198
Coke-oven products.............	11 cir	20,603	2,041A	1,607	1,230A	17,350	11,510A	4,097	3,365A
Trunks, suitcases, bags, etc......	?	8,708	*	971	*	4,446	*	2,088	*
Cement.......................	4 cir	26,426	1,015A	1,289	1,045A	6,933	7,120A	4,284	4,250A
Clay products..................	18.9	59,585	11,237	971	686	2,740	2,162	1,884	1,407
Concrete products..............	13.5	12,840	1,735	1,073	787	5,933	4,250	3,171	2,220
Glass.........................	4 cir	79,051	511T	1,285	*	4,905	*	3,125	*
Wall and insulation board, etc.....	10 cir	6,383	*	1,048	*	6,431	*	3,979	*
Blast-furnace products...........	10 cir	23,075	1,831A	1,647	1,394A	29,145	21,625A	5,532	6,175A
Boiler shop products.............	10 cir	24,485	1,164T	1,382	1,131T	6,750	4,510T	3,361	2,121T
Foundry products...............	4.0	120,024	4,754	1,321	964	3,310	3,082	2,129	1,877
Heating and cooking apparatus...	9.7	89,287	8,642	1,252	865	4,920	2,724	2,903	1,558
Steel barrels and kegs............	5 cir	6,231	204L	1,181	895L	7,732	12,580L	2,869	3,600L
Structural steel, etc.............	9.6	38,814	3,745	1,389	1,105	7,542	6,327	3,171	2,652
Rolling mill products............	4 cir	479,342	11,242A	1,627	*	6,948	*	3,123	*
Ship building..................	18 cir	62,474	7,464V	1,505	*	4,022	*	2,393	*
Brooms.......................	18.4	4,067	750	714	525	2,859	2,114	1,310	994
Mattresses and bedsprings.......	14.6	19,165	2,789	1,034	782	5,902	4,884	2,605	2,112

*No data. †Louisiana probably has more wage earners.

Key to abbreviations: A, Alabama; F, Florida; L, Louisiana: SC, South Carolina; T, Tennessee; V, Virginia. The state with the largest number of wage earners is used as a sample of the Southeast when regional data are unavailable.

The indices for the industries in which the Southeast has the resources and skills to manufacture for the region are recapitulated here for convenience in reference. Columnar arrangement makes it possible to compare any one item of all industries better than can be done with the individual industry tables in the text.

The contrasts of these industries with Group I are significant. Considering first the United States' columns, only 8 industries have wages per wage earner of less than $1,000, many are near the national average of $1,180 and 18 are above. In value of product this group includes a dozen of the highest index industries in the United States, an indication of their capacity as users of raw materials. In value added by manufacture half of the industries are above the national average of $2,938 and only 2 are seriously below that figure, men's shirts and brooms. The number of wage earners per salaried person is strikingly lower than in Group I and the salary expenditure per wage earner correspondingly larger, showing the greater employment opportunity for technical and clerical workers. The balance

The remaining 28 might well be encouraged. All have from average to high wage indices. Few require high capital investment and their value added by manufacture is sufficient to provide a margin for taxes and return on capital after wages and salaries are paid. They represent fields of manufacturing using a wide range of agricultural, forest and mineral resources. They produce articles which the region uses. Increases would help balance, not only merely the manufacturing, but the entire production economy of the region.

MANUFACTURING FOR THE REGION

Group II Industries

Percent wages are of value added by mfr.		Salary per salaried person		Salary per wage earner		Wage earners per salaried person		Wage and salary per wage earner		Percent wages and salary are of value added by mfr.		Balance per wage earner, for interest, profits, taxes, etc.	
U.S.	S.E.	U.S.	S.E.	U.S.	S.E.	U.S.	S.E.	U.S.	S.E.	U.S.	S.E.	U.S.	S.E.
42.0	37.9	1,914	1,713	190	182	10.1	9.5	1,415	1,137	48.4	44.9	1,507	1,393
31.9	33.9	1,840	1,395	146	75	12.6	18.6	822	432	38.9	41.0	1,296	622
35.2	29.8	2,106	1,922	216	241	9.8	8.0	1,025	862	44.7	41.4	1,266	1,219
20.6	18.2	1,804	1,744	600	613	3.0	2.8	1,700	1,321	32.0	33.8	3,628	2,583
19.8	18.8	2,170	2,122	453	350	4.8	6.1	1,368	932	29.5	30.2	3,266	2,152
15.4	16.9	1,911	1,839	597	697	3.2	2.6	1,737	1,589	23.4	30.2	5,679	3,684
16.1	20.5T	2,030	2,118T	498	365T	4.1	5.8T	1,648	1,237T	23.0	29.1T	5,512	3,013T
33.5	36.5L	2,852	1,860L	358	301L	8.0	6.2L	1,295	663L	46.3	66.7L	1,500	329L
48.4	68.8SC	1,800	1,296SC	103	71SC	17.4	18.3SC	732	515SC	56.4	68.2SC	566	240SC
37.8	36.6	2,081	2,034	586	640	3.5	3.2	1,610	1,601	59.5	60.8	1,098	1,025
39.7	46.0	2,414	2,321	426	330	5.7	7.1	1,531	1,127	54.9	65.2	1,257	600
36.3	24.9V	2,714	3,043V	287	329V	9.4	9.2V	1,569	1,470V	44.5	32.1V	1,955	3,110V
38.5	24.6L	2,512	2,809L	344	374L	7.3	7.5L	1,357	1,214L	51.7	35.5L	1,267	2,206L
37.2	40.4	2,293	1,980	702	533	3.3	3.7	2,082	1,685	55.9	59.2	1,640	1,170
44.7	*	2,393	*	409	*	5.8	*	1,541	*	60.9	*	988	*
23.3	30.0	2,682	3,175	252	135	10.6	23.4	1,490	1,193	28.1	33.8	3,815	2,339
24.5	18.2	2,584	2,295	552	371	4.7	6.2	2,037	1,547	33.7	23.9	4,013	4,916
15.6	15.4V	2,056	1,781V	674	746V	3.0	2.4V	2,090	1,921V	23.1	25.1V	6,970	5,704V
10.5	8.8	2,324	2,002	949	1,055	2.4	1.9	2,033	1,787	19.8	21.5	8,222	6,516
12.5	20.8F	2,314	1,980F	1,314	584F	1.8	3.4F	2,392	1,151F	27.9	42.3F	6,184	1,569F
22.1	38.3V	2,652	1,774V	580	370V	4.6	4.8V	1,777	1,260V	32.9	54.2V	3,625	1,062V
18.9	17.0	2,378	2,670	901	1,090	2.6	2.4	2,251	2,140	31.5	34.6	4,898	4,058
39.2	36.6A	2,698	2,660A	276	225A	9.8	11.8A	1,883	1,455A	46.0	43.2A	2,214	1,910A
46.4	*	2,166	*	249	*	8.7	*	1,220	*	58.4	*	868	*
30.1	24.6A	2,467	2,743A	252	265A	9.8	10.4A	1,541	1,310A	36.0	30.8A	2,743	2,940A
51.5	48.8	2,102	2,272	172	150	12.2	15.2	1,143	836	60.7	59.4	741	571
33.9	35.4	2,046	1,966	390	342	5.2	5.8	1,463	1,129	46.1	50.8	1,708	1,091
41.1	*	2,238	*	225	*	9.9	*	1,510	*	48.3	*	1,615	*
26.5	*	1,824	*	274	*	6.7	*	1,322	*	33.2	*	2,657	*
29.8	22.6A	2,945	2,315A	237	188A	12.4	12.3A	1,884	1,582A	34.0	25.6A	3,648	4,593A
41.2	53.3T	2,224	2,822T	493	245T	4.5	11.5T	1,875	1,376T	55.8	64.8T	1,486	745T
62.1	51.3	2,501	2,076	189	234	13.3	8.8	1,510	1,198	70.9	63.8	619	679
43.1	55.5	2,127	2,249	340	153	6.3	14.7	1,592	1,018	54.8	65.3	1,311	540
41.2	24.9L	2,198	1,538L	289	188L	7.6	8.1L	1,470	1,083L	51.2	30.1L	1,399	2,517L
43.7	41.6	2,342	2,303	522	534	4.5	4.3	1,911	1,639	60.3	61.8	1,260	1,013
52.0	*	2,694	*	228	*	11.8	*	1,855	*	59.4	*	1,268	*
63.0	*	2,526	*	309	*	8.2	*	1,814	*	75.8	*	579	*
54.5	52.9	1,580	1,265	148	108	10.6	11.7	862	633	65.8	63.7	448	361
39.7	37.0	2,094	2,451	346	344	6.0	7.1	1,380	1,126	53.0	53.3	1,225	986

for interest, profits, taxes, etc., is below $1,000 in 7 of the 39 industries compared with 23 of the 44 industries in Group I. In 22 of these industries it is above, and in 13 more than twice the national average. Altogether this is not a poor showing for a group which includes only two or three highly skilled industries.

The indices for the portion of these industries in the Southeast, or the sample states when regional figures are unavailable, are considerably lower than for each industry as a whole. But, in general, they are considerably better than the Southeastern average for all industries. In 10 of the 33 for which a comparative figure is available, the wage per wage earner is lower than the regional average, but in most of these cases the percent of the value added which is expended in wages seems to indicate that higher wages would be possible if necessary to secure workers. In 25 of the 33 the value added by manufacture is above and in 10 cases double the regional average ($1,987). The opportunity for technical and clerical workers is obvious in the low number of wage earners per salaried person: in only 5 industries is the number larger than the regional average (12.5) and in 15 cases it is even smaller than the national average (7).

CHAPTER IV

MANUFACTURING FOR REGIONAL BALANCE—GROUP III INDUSTRIES

The Southeast manufactures cheaply some of its most abundant raw materials into cheap products for the nation. This is a contribution to the national economy. Although the rise of these industries (discussed as Group I in Chapter II) has greatly aided the South, they are not numerous enough nor do they pay wages nor create values high enough for balanced production.

The Southeast manufactures some of its lesser resources and processes further some of its crude manufactured products. It should do more—at least enough to supply its proportional part on the basis of population. Many of the industries in this class (Group II, Chapter III) pay good wages and create high values.

But even if planning boards and chambers of commerce could interest entrepreneurs in building all these, there would still remain a great source of regional unbalance: an agriculture based on a few commercial crops in which there is serious overproduction. Leaders in the South have preached diversification for generations and active programs have been in progress for over a decade. Southern farmers have long been used to markets for these old crops at the nearest town. If a few diversify they can, with some trouble, peddle their products to stores and homes. But a farmer who could sell a hundred bales of cotton any morning—at some price—can glut his little market for turnip greens from a three acre patch. If all are to diversify they must have ready markets, not the sort of system by which a dozen farmers must arrange to contribute their chickens to make up a single carload going to a packing house three hundred miles away or to a big city even farther away. The farmer is used to gambling on the market; he should not be expected to gamble on it when he knows there is no market; in this respect at least he has some of the perspicacity of the industrialist. Canneries and pickle factories scattered over the Southeast have proved that the surrounding farmers will raise such an unaccustomed crop as tomatoes or peppers or dill if they are reasonably sure it will not be left to rot in the fields. The building of plants for evaporating and condensing milk has changed the dominant form of agriculture in some counties. Planning for optimum production in manufacturing in the Southeast, then, should include developments that will aid in regional balance and optimum production in agriculture.

This third group of industries, accordingly, includes many that thrive as small local establishments, thus scattering markets among the producers. Most are users of large amounts of raw material per wage earner (roughly measured by the difference between the value of product and the value added by manufacture). In many of these industries the region has had some experience, and besides, they require only a small number of technical and skilled workers. Most are high index industries and so are desirable on their own account. This is a group of industries which the Southeast should encourage, at least to the point of supplying its own needs, in order to add variety and balance to its manufacturing and help to balance its agricultural economy as well.

INDUSTRIES USING AGRICULTURAL PRODUCTS

Flour and Other Grain Milling. Several of these center around increase in field crops. For example, the bread and bakery products and the prepared animal feed industries, discussed in Chapter III, can be increased somewhat in the Southeast now, but to bring the region's share up to the population ratio out of its own raw materials, more grain must be grown and more flour and other mills established. Because of the type of machinery and processing involved, milling requires considerable capital: the capital assets of eight large companies average between $8,000 and $10,000 per wage earner. The balance left for interest, etc., however, is adequate. Skill requirements are also considerable; skilled workmen and foremen make up 30 percent of all persons attached to the industry, compared with 22 percent for all manufacturing and from 4 to 10 percent for most of the industries located mainly in the Southeast. The demands for technical skill on the professional level are not so large: 0.8 percent of the entire personnel as compared with 1.5 percent for all manufacturing

FLOUR AND OTHER GRAIN MILL PRODUCTS	United States	Southeast	Percent
Number of wage earners	26,390	3,819	14.5
Wage per wage earner	$ 1,144	$ 763	66.7
Value of product per wage earner	$32,448	$20,278	62.5
Value added by manufacture per wage earner	$ 5,063	$ 3,358	66.3
Percent wages are of value added by manufacture	22.6	22.7	
Salary per salaried person	$ 2,098	$ 1,911	91.1
Salary per wage earner	$ 525	$ 417	79.4
Number of wage earners per salaried person	4.0	4.6	115.0
Wage and salary per wage earner	$ 1,669	$ 1,180	70.7
Percent wage and salary are of value added by manufacture	32.9	35.2	
Balance for interest, profits, taxes	$ 3,394	$ 2,178	64.2

and 2.3 percent in rayon and 3.2 in sugar factories and refineries.[1] Flour and other grain milling has experienced decreases since 1925. The region now has 14.5 percent of the wage earners in the industry. The expenditure for salaries and wages takes only a little more than one-third the value added instead of two-thirds as do many southern industries.

Malt and Malt Liquors. Malt and malt liquors, two of the most rapidly growing industries in the country, are based on grain crops. It used to be said that the South, with a minimum of population of German background, cared little for beers. Casual attention to roadside signs of beer sellers is sufficient to show that this is no longer true. The region has only 5.8 percent of the wage earners in the large malt liquor industry and none in the small malt industry. Capital requirements appear to be around $6,000 per wage earner. These two rank among the highest index industries in the United States. The figures for the first are given here; those for malt are even higher.[2]

MALT LIQUORS	United States	South-east	Per-cent
Number of wage earners	47,037	2,706	5.8
Wage per wage earner	$ 1,685	$ 1,360	80.7
Value of product per wage earner	$11,419	$ 7,783	68.2
Value added by manufacture per wage earner	$ 7,126	$ 4,967	69.7
Percent wages are of value added by manufacture	23.6	27.4	
Salary per salaried person	$ 2,510	$ 2,090	
Salary per wage earner	$ 554	$ 474	85.6
Number of wage earners per salaried person	4.5	4.4	97.8
Wage and salary per wage earner	$ 2,239	$ 1,834	81.9
Percent wage and salary are of value added by manufacture	31.4	37.0	
Balance for interest, profits, taxes	$ 4,887	$ 3,133	64.0

Corn Sirup, Starch, etc. Another high index industry based on grains is corn sirup, sugar, oil, and starch. Here the Southeast lacks a single plant. Statistics for this as a separate industry go back only to 1933. Since that time there have been decreases in the number of wage earners and the value added by manufacture. The detailed figures are not given here though they are included in the summary table at the end of the chapter.

Dairy Products. For expansion in the region several industries in this group require as raw material more dairy and basic livestock products. All these have high value of product per wage earner, showing them to be

BUTTER	United States	South-east	Per-cent
Number of wage earners	19,437	927	4.8
Wage per wage earner	$ 1,009	$ 820	81.3
Value of product per wage earner	$30,342	$24,277	80.0
Value added by manufacture per wage earner	$ 4,100	$ 4,206	102.6
Percent wages are of value added by manufacture	24.6	19.5	
Salary per salaried person	$ 1,403	$ 1,461	104.1
Salary per wage earner	$ 472	$ 557	118.0
Number of wage earners per salaried person	3.0	2.6	86.7
Wage and salary per wage earner	$ 1,481	$ 1,377	93.0
Percent wage and salary are of value added by manufacture	36.4	32.7	
Balance for interest, profits, taxes	$ 3,619	$ 2,829	78.2

[1] See table in Chapter V.   [2] Indices in table at end of chapter.

enormous markets for raw material. One, ice cream, has already been discussed in Chapter III. Other dairy products are processed in similarly high index industries and all show wide manufacturing margins. The region has 4.8 percent of the wage earners in butter making. The industry increased 9.4 percent in wage earners between 1925 and 1937, but experienced small decreases by other measures.

Cheese manufacturing is a much smaller industry than butter and has a lower wage index, though its high value added by manufacture leaves large enough margin to afford better wages if necessary. As an employer of labor it is growing rapidly, having increased in number of wage earners 31.9 percent between 1925 and 1937, though increases in other factors are smaller.

Cheese	United States	Southeast	Percent
Number of wage earners	4,482	262	5.8
Wage per wage earner	$ 973	$ 821	84.4
Value of product per wage earner	$25,164	$18,103	71.9
Value added by manufacture per wage earner	$ 3,818	$ 3,382	88.6
Percent wages are of value added by manufacture	25.5	24.0	
Salary per salaried person	$ 1,464	$ 1,051	71.8
Salary per wage earner	$ 204	$ 261	127.9
Number of wage earners per salaried person	7.2	4.0	55.6
Wage and salary per wage earner	$ 1,177	$ 1,077	91.5
Percent wage and salary are of value added by manufacture	30.8	31.8	
Balance for interest, profits, taxes	$ 2,641	$ 2,305	87.4

Regional figures for the evaporated and condensed milk industry are not available, but the Southeast has about 10 percent of the wage earners. Sample indices for one state, Tennessee, suggest that the portion in the Southeast comes nearer attaining the average for the whole industry than any other branch of dairy products manufacture. The total number of wage earners in the industry increased 26 percent, value of product, 23 percent, and value added by manufacture 42 percent between 1925 and 1937.

Evaporated and Condensed Milk	United States	Tennessee	Percent
Number of wage earners	8,967	244	
Wage per wage earner	$ 1,110	$ 940	84.7
Value of product per wage earner	$23,600	$17,550	74.4
Value added by manufacture per wage earner	$ 4,930	$ 4,230	85.8
Percent wages are of value added by manufacture	22.5	22.2	
Salary per salaried person	$ 1,852	$ 1,895	102.3
Salary per wage earner	$ 367	$ 233	63.5
Number of wage earners per salaried person	5.0	8.1	162.0
Wage and salary per wage earner	$ 1,477	$ 1,173	79.4
Percent wage and salary are of value added by manufacture	30.0	27.9	
Balance for interest, profits, taxes	$ 3,453	$ 3,057	88.5

Even the usual rough estimates of capital requirements for specific dairy products industries are unsatisfactory because most companies manufacture several of these products and sell milk as well. It seems likely that capital costs average around $5,000 per wage earner. The balance for interest, etc. is adequate for that investment.

Meat Packing. Meat packing is the fifteenth industry in the United States in size. The Southeast has only 5.6 percent of the 127,000 wage earners. Wages per wage earner are considerably lower in the Southeast than for the whole industry but are better than for most industries in the region. Its value added by manufacture and balance for interest, etc. are only average considering the capital investment of around $5,000 per wage earner. Its chief advantage to the region would be as a market for large quantities of the products of livestock raising, a phase of agricultural development much needed in the Southeast. Secondary and by-products would supply raw materials for several desirable smaller industries. Decreases in value of product and value added by manufacture between 1925 and 1937 are partially accounted for by differences in price levels; it is, however, a stationary or decreasing rather than a growing industry.

MEAT PACKING, WHOLESALE	United States	Southeast	Percent
Number of wage earners	127,477	7,161	5.6
Wage per wage earner	$ 1,337	$ 930	69.6
Value of product per wage earner	$21,866	$14,692	67.2
Value added by manufacture per wage earner	$ 3,148	$ 2,467	78.4
Percent wages are of value added by manufacture	42.4	37.8	
Salary per salaried person	$ 2,084	$ 1,992	95.6
Salary per wage earner	$ 411	$ 348	84.7
Number of wage earners per salaried person	5.1	5.7	111.8
Wage and salary per wage earner	$ 1,748	$ 1,278	73.1
Percent wage and salary are of value added by manufacture	55.5	52.0	
Balance for interest, profits, taxes	$ 1,400	$ 1,189	84.9

Poultry Dressing. About four percent of the wage earners in the poultry dressing and packing industry are found in the Southeast. By most indices this is a low industry, though the small expenditure for wage and salary results in a larger margin than in many industries in the region. Like meat packing it would be less valuable on its own account as an industry for the Southeast than as a market for large quantities of farm produce.

POULTRY DRESSING	United States	Tennessee	Percent
Number of wage earners	8,913	183	
Wage per wage earner	$ 666	$ 536	80.5
Value of product per wage earner	$11,870	$11,380	95.9
Value added by manufacture per wage earner	$ 2,050	$ 1,560	76.1
Percent wages are of value added by manufacture	32.5	35.4	
Salary per salaried person	$ 1,580	$ 1,484	93.9
Salary per wage earner	$ 219	$ 195	89.0
Number of wage earners per salaried person	7.2	7.6	105.6
Wage and salary per wage earner	$ 855	$ 721	84.3
Percent wage and salary are of value added by manufacture	43.2	46.3	
Balance for interest, profits, taxes	$ 1,165	$ 839	72.0

Sausage, etc. The sausage, meat puddings, etc. industry as a whole has high indices; in a sample state in the Southeast it is low in wages ($776), better than average in value added by manufacture ($2,215) and in its

MANUFACTURING FOR REGIONAL BALANCE

balance left for interest, etc. ($1,534). Its high value of product ($15,-410) shows it, like those just discussed, to be a great user of raw materials.[8]

Miscellaneous Food Preparations. One other food industry, miscellaneous food preparations, was regarded in Chapter III as capable of some expansion with present resources. Any considerable growth in this branch would call for increased production of many of the same field and animal crops required in the larger food industries already discussed. This is a low wage industry, but high in value added by manufacture, and wages and salaries account for less than one-third of the value added. The industry increased its wage earners 87.9 percent from 1931 to 1937. Made up as it is of many types of ready-to-serve foods, the products of this composite industry will be in increasing demand in the South in view of the growing trend toward light housekeeping and apartment life, and of married women working outside the home.

Miscellaneous food preparations	United States	Southeast	Percent
Number of wage earners	16,794	1,450	8.6
Wage per wage earner	$ 915	$ 582	63.6
Value of product per wage earner	$16,592	$11,584	69.8
Value added by manufacture per wage earner	$ 4,634	$ 3,084	66.6
Percent wages are of value added by manufacture	19.8	18.8	
Salary per salaried person	$ 2,170	$ 2,122	97.8
Salary per wage earner	$ 453	$ 350	77.3
Number of wage earners per salaried person	4.8	6.1	127.1
Wage and salary per wage earner	$ 1,368	$ 932	68.1
Percent wage and salary are of value added by manufacture	29.5	30.2	
Balance for interest, profits, taxes	$ 3,266	$ 2,152	65.9

Miscellaneous Animal Products. Several other industries, most of them desirable in themselves, should be encouraged in order to provide markets for additional resources in animal products. Among them are carpet yarn, wool carpets, grease and tallow, soap, leather, and boots and shoes. There are plenty of textile workers in the region whose skills would require only slight training for the first two in the list. Incidentally, work in rug and carpet mills does not suffer from nearly so marked a social stigma as that in cotton mills. The pattern setting departments, in particular, are so respectable that they have been known to attract the class of girls who usually prefer lower wages at sales and clerical work to factory employ-

	CARPETS, WOOL	CARPET YARN
Number of wage earners in the United States	30,779	2,584
Wage per wage earner	$ 1,045	$ 1,151
Value of product per wage earner	$ 5,207	$ 6,521
Value added by manufacture per wage earner	$ 2,554	$ 1,975
Percent wages are of value added by manufacture	41.0	58.3
Salary per salaried person	$ 2,184	$ 3,398
Salary per wage earner	$ 163	$ 189
Number of wage earners per salaried person	13.4	17.9
Wage and salary per wage earner	$ 1,208	$ 1,340
Percent wage and salary are of value added by manufacture	47.3	67.8
Balance for interest, profits, taxes	$ 1,346	$ 635

[8] Indices in table at end of chapter.

ment. A large proportion of the low value added by manufacture is absorbed by wages and salaries, but the balance is still larger than that found in most textile industries. The Southeast has no establishment making carpet yarn and only about three percent of the wage earners in the wool carpet industry. There are no statistics for individual southeastern states and so the United States indices for the two industries are given together.

Grease and tallow, though small as a separate industry, uses large quantities of raw materials per wage earner chiefly in the form of by-products of meat packing. It shows average, or better, indices. There are few plants in the Southeast, employing probably two percent of the total wage earners. The much larger soap industry uses greases as well as rosin discussed in Chapter II. It is well above average on all scores; high wage, enormous use of raw materials per wage earner, and high value added by manufacture of which wages and salaries absorb less than one-fourth. This leaves a large balance, even considering its high capital investment of probably close to $10,000 per wage earner. Between 1925 and 1937 value of product increased 8 percent and value added by manufacture, 24 percent. The Southeast has only some two percent of the wage earners in this industry. Since there are no satisfactory statistics for the region or state these two are also shown together.

	GREASE AND TALLOW	SOAP
Number of wage earners in the United States	5,200	14,008
Wage per wage earner	$ 1,301	$ 1,362
Value of product per wage earner	$10,052	$21,508
Value added by manufacture per wage earner	$ 3,709	$ 8,290
Percent wages are of value added by manufacture	35.0	16.4
Salary per salaried person	$ 2,573	$ 2,128
Salary per wage earner	$ 434	$ 550
Number of wage earners per salaried person	5.9	3.9
Wage and salary per wage earner	$ 1,735	$ 1,912
Percent wage and salary are of value added by manufacture	46.8	23.1
Balance for interest, profits, taxes	$ 1,974	$ 6,378

An important by-product of animal husbandry and meat packing is leather and the industry next in order of processing, boots and shoes. The Southeast, for all its traditional bare feet, certainly uses more of the products of these two industries than are produced by the five percent of the wage earners employed in the region. Leather, tanned and curried, is an industry of high indices in all except balance left for interest, etc. The boot and shoe industry, though low, is better than many of the large industries already in the region. Both require little technically trained personnel (0.6 percent and 0.3 percent respectively) and large numbers of semiskilled and unskilled workers.[4]

Linseed Oil. One other industry of the chemical group is included here as a possible development in the Southeast, linseed oil. At present the region has none of the industry and produces none of the raw materials

[4] For indices of these two industries see table at end of chapter.

—flaxseed. The new cigarette paper factory established in Transylvania County, North Carolina, which makes the paper direct from flax instead of rags, is already being hailed as furnishing a market for a new crop. Linseed oil processing would enlarge this market. It is a high wage industry, ($1,367) uses great amounts of raw materials per wage earner (value of product, $34,382) and has a value added by manufacture ($6,041) twice as high as the average for all industries in the United States. Wages and salaries absorb only 26.0 percent of the value added, compared with about 50 percent in all industries combined, leaving $4,470 balance for interest, etc.[5] The main product of this industry, linseed oil, is necessary for expansion of the equally desirable paint industry discussed in Chapter III; its by-products, meal and cake, are important ingredients of the prepared animal feed industry. Linseed oil is also an important material for three other industries highly desirable for the Southeast, artificial leather, asphalted-felt-base floor covering and linoleum.

Artificial Leather, Linoleum, etc. These three industries used in the neighborhood of two hundred million square yards of textile fabrics in 1937. They use, besides linseed and other oils, solvents producible in the chemical industries of the region, wood flour, clay and other fillers. The cork used in asphalted-felt-base coverings has to be imported from abroad no matter where the industry is located. Statistics on growth earlier than 1931 are unavailable in the census, but between 1931 and 1937 they increased as follows:

	Percent Increase 1931-1937		
	Number of wage earners	Value of product	Value added by manufacture
Artificial leather	30.9	81.7	50.4
Asphalted-felt-base floor covering	68.6	67.8	46.8
Linoleum	66.7	55.0	34.7

All three are high index industries. Data on capital requirements are meager, but the assets of four companies employing the majority of the workers in these industries average $7,100 per wage earner. Balances left for interest, etc., range from adequate to high.

	ARTIFICIAL LEATHER	ASPHALTED FLOOR COVERING	LINOLEUM
Number of wage earners in the United States	2,541	3,280	4,827
Wage per wage earner	$ 1,368	$ 1,455	$1,368
Value of product per wage earner	$10,865	$10,228	$7,383
Value added by manufacture per wage earner	$ 3,618	$ 4,853	4,218
Percent wages are of value added by manufacture	37.8	30.0	32.4
Salary per salaried person	$ 2,840	$ 2,658	$2,077
Salary per wage earner	$ 452	$ 230	$ 190
Number of wage earners per salaried person	6.3	11.5	10.9
Wage and salary per wage earner	$ 1,820	$ 1,685	$1,558
Percent wage and salary are of value added by manufacture	50.4	34.7	37.0
Balance for interest, profits, taxes	$ 1,798	$ 3,168	$2,660

[5] Indices in table at end of chapter.

OTHER INDUSTRIES

Lithographing and Photoengraving. Two industries in the printing and publishing group, lithographing and photoengraving, are included in this list as desirable and possible chiefly because the region has a considerably larger percent of the printing industries which form a market for their custom work than it has of these two. The Southeast has 8.9 percent of the wage earners in newspapers and periodicals and 6.2 percent in book and job printing as compared with 4.5 percent in photoengraving and about 2 percent in lithographing. These industries have grown rapidly since 1933, an unsatisfactory base for comparison but the first year for which separate statistics are available. They are highly skilled industries and the region would undoubtedly be obliged to import skills in order to expand the small beginnings in the Southeast.

	LITHO-GRAPHING	PHOTO-ENGRAVING
Number of wage earners in the United States	24,079	12,364
Wage per wage earner	$ 1,492	$ 2,355
Value of product per wage earner	$ 5,721	$ 6,305
Value added by manufacture per wage earner	$ 3,464	$ 5,068
Percent wages are of value added by manufacture	43.1	46.4
Salary per salaried person	$ 2,754	$ 2,778
Salary per wage earner	$ 663	$ 1,020
Number of wage earners per salaried person	4.2	2.7
Wage and salary per wage earner	$ 2,155	$ 3,375
Percent wage and salary are of value added by manufacture	62.2	66.6
Balance for interest, profits, taxes	$ 1,309	$ 1,693

Pottery. A natural resource of the southern states which has been much talked of, and cited as the basis for possible industries, is clay for pottery making. One industry using this resource is summarized here, pottery and porcelain including bathroom fixtures. This requires technical skill, but in small enough amounts to make its importation easy; mainly it is carried on with large amounts of semiskilled and unskilled labor. The region has a small start with probably three percent of the wage earners. This is not a high index industry, and not greatly desirable except on the general principle of giving variety to manufactures, supplying the regional market with bulky goods in general use, and using natural resources. It has experienced decreases in number of wage earners, in value of product and in value added by manufacture since 1925. General revival in building will, of course, aid this industry.

POTTERY AND PORCELAIN (INCL. BATHROOM FIXTURES)	United States
Number of wage earners	33,060
Wage per wage earner	$ 1,159
Value of product per wage earner	$ 2,865
Value added by manufacture per wage earner	$ 2,071
Percent wages are of value added by manufacture	56.0
Salary per salaried person	$ 2,467
Salary per wage earner	$ 196
Number of wage earners per salaried person	12.6
Wage and salary per wage earner	$ 1,355
Percent wage and salary are of value added by manufacture	65.4
Balance for interest, profits, taxes	$ 716

Iron and Steel Industries. As noted in Chapter III, local encouragement of iron and steel manufacture is difficult because of the corporate structure of the industry. Also consideration of separate industries in this group is difficult and misleading because of the large amounts of the products made in vertically organized establishments. Four of these separate industries are included here chiefly as illustrations of the types of products, rather than definite industries, in which expansion in the Southeast might be made. Three of the four are high wage industries but are not particularly high in other respects. Over half of the value added by manufacture per wage earner is expended in wages and salaries, leaving a relatively small balance for interest, profits, taxes, etc. It is claimed by the American Iron and Steel Institute that an investment of $10,000 per wage earner is necessary in the industry as a whole. Unless the capital requirements are considerably smaller for these subdivisions, the balance left after interest on investment is decidedly unfavorable.

	BOLTS AND NUTS *	FORGING*
Number of wage earners in the United States	16,840	18,255
Wage per wage earner	$ 1,312	$ 1,515
Value of product per wage earner	$ 5,824	$ 6,729
Value added by manufacture per wage earner	$ 3,191	$ 3,265
Percent wages are of value added by manufacture	41.1	46.4
Salary per salaried person	$ 2,641	$ 3,100
Salary per wage earner	$ 359	$ 336
Number of wage earners per salaried person	7.4	9.2
Wage and salary per wage earner	$ 1,671	$ 1,851
Percent wage and salary are of value added by manufacture	52.4	56.7
Balance for interest, profits, taxes	$ 1,520	$ 1,414

*Not made in rolling mills.

	WIRE	WIRE WORK N.E.C.
Number of wage earners in the United States	24,580	33,471
Wage per wage earner	$ 1,382	$ 1,171
Value of product per wage earner	$ 7,329	$ 4,915
Value added by manufacture per wage earner	$ 3,327	$ 2,576
Percent wages are of value added by manufacture	41.5	45.5
Salary per salaried person	$ 2,530	$ 2,577
Salary per wage earner	$ 326	$ 339
Number of wage earners per salaried person	7.8	7.6
Wage and salary per wage earner	$ 1,708	$ 1,510
Percent wage and salary are of value added by manufacture	51.3	58.6
Balance for interest, profits, taxes	$ 1,619	$ 1,066

Miscellaneous Industries. There are a number of other industries possible and desirable. Some process additional by-products, as glue and gelatin or oleomargarine. Others further process products already at hand, as window and door screens, etc. or synthetic resin, cellulose-plastics, and others using chemicals, iron and steel and aluminum. Still others are accessory industries, as tin plate, tin cans and tin foil.[6]

[6] For indices see table in Chapter VI.

Selected Industries With High Value of Product Per Wage Earner

Industry	Total wage earners	Wages per wage earner	Value of product per wage earner	Value added by manufacture per wage earner	Percent of wage earners in Southeast
Butter	19,437	$ 1,009	$30,342	$ 4,110	4.8
Cheese	4,482	973	25,164	3,818	5.8
Evaporated and condensed milk	8,967	1,110	23,600	4,930	*10.0 cir*
Corn sirup, etc., and starch	7,010	1,490	19,300	5,610	0
Feeds, prepared, animal and fowl	14,397	1,100	28,840	5,328	12.5
Flavoring extracts	4,162	1,030	28,300	17,200	*12.0 cir*
Flour and other grain mill products	26,390	1,144	32,448	5,063	14.5
Foods not elsewhere classified (prepared)	16,794	915	16,592	4,634	8.6
Ice cream	18,664	1,140	15,109	7,416	12.8
Liquors, distilled	6,215	1,193	18,198	6,420	34.1
Liquors, malt	47,037	1,685	11,419	7,126	5.8
Liquors, rectified and blended	7,094	949	20,363	10,160	4.1
Malt	1,644	1,770	57,189	11,250	0
Meat packing	127,477	1,337	21,866	3,148	5.6
Oleomargarine, not made in meating packing ests	1,214	1,320	36,800	11,160	0
Poultry dressing and packing	8,913	666	11,870	2,050	*4.0 cir*
Sausage, meat pudding, etc	9,342	1,220	16,000	3,240	*8.0 cir*
Shortening and oils, vegetable—not lard	4,901	1,150	48,862	7,160	*15.0 cir*
Sugar refining	14,024	1,140	30,200	4,410	*27.0 cir*
Bags other than paper	12,075	807	10,766	2,176	*30.0 cir*
Artificial leather	2,541	1,368	10,865	3,618	0
Oilcloth	1,269	1,338	10,100	2,713	0
Asphalted-felt-base floor covering	3,280	1,455	10,228	4,853	0
Coke-oven products	20,603	1,607	17,350	4,097	*11.0 cir*
Lubricating oil, not made in refineries	2,231	1,273	19,773	8,393	*2.0 cir*
Petroleum refining	83,182	1,688	30,616	5,800	*6.0 cir*
Blast-furnace products	23,075	1,647	29,145	5,532	*10.0 cir*
Tin cans and other tinware	33,145	1,122	10,825	3,430	*4.0 cir*
Baking powder	2,380	1,580	12,722	7,122	*3.0 cir*
Blackings, stains and dressings	1,536	963	12,489	7,288	*6.0 cir*
Chemicals, industrial, not elsewhere classified	78,951	1,485	11,814	6,050	9.7
Cleaning and polishing preparations	3,341	1,180	17,322	10,285	*1.0 cir*
Compressed and liquefied gases	4,655	1,416	12,120	9,060	*7.0 cir*
Drugs and medicines	24,095	1,084	14,356	10,255	5.5
Explosives	5,406	1,595	10,762	6,284	*1.0 cir*
Glue and gelatin	3,547	1,287	11,460	4,866	*1.0 cir*
Grease and tallow	5,200	1,301	10,052	3,709	*2.0 cir*
Ink, printing	2,793	1,463	16,952	7,964	*1.5 cir*
Insecticides	4,322	1,078	16,467	8,576	*10.0 cir*
Oils not elsewhere classified	2,474	1,197	28,083	5,402	*10.0 cir*
Paints, pigments, and varnishes	31,664	1,350	17,005	7,149	4.7
Soap	14,008	1,362	21,509	8,290	*2.0 cir*
Linseed oil and cake	2,628	1,367	34,382	6,041	0
Tinfoil, etc	1,669	1,410	10,641	3,956	?
Roofing, asphalt shingles	7,418	1,283	13,826	5,381	*3.0 cir*
Paving material, blocks, etc	1,946	1,243	12,995	5,490	*

Selected Industries With Low Value of Product Per Wage Earner

Industry	Total wage earners	Wages per wage earner	Value of product per wage earner	Value added by manufacture per wage earner	Percent of wage earners in Southeast
Cotton woven goods	336,104	761	2,877	1,313	74.0
Cotton yarn and thread	86,206	659	3,023	1,224	78.5
Dyeing and finishing cotton fabrics	49,635	987	4,111	1,972	*34.0 cir*
Dyeing and finishing cotton yarn	7,344	944	2,943	2,015	*35.0 cir*
Hosiery	150,460	906	2,403	1,340	44.2
Knitted underwear	39,923	715	2,950	1,361	33.3
Rayon woven goods	57,949	845	3,965	1,391	36.0
Men's and boys' work clothing	69,502	594	2,941	1,029	35.3
Men's and boys' trousers, wash suits	15,817	603	2,957	1,081	*25.0 cir*
Men's and boys' shirts (not work)	55,570	629	3,149	1,298	*13.0 cir*
Men's and boys' underwear	7,888	534	2,572	834	*18.0 cir*
Baskets and willow ware	9,308	551	1,789	1,041	*39.0 cir*
Boxes, cigar	3,296	704	2,163	1,349	*26.0 cir*
Boxes, wooden	25,981	752	3,323	1,574	39.6
Excelsior	960	760	3,160	1,769	*23.0 cir*
Furniture	130,765	947	3,614	1,855	22.7
Lumber and timber	323,928	849	2,619	1,555	44.5
Wood, turned and shaped	23,087	844	3,044	1,621	27.4
Clay products (not pottery)	59,585	971	2,740	1,884	18.9
Lime	9,751	986	3,592	2,229	*24.0 cir*
Marble, granite, etc	20,816	1,171	3,795	2,482	22.5
Cast iron pipe	17,613	1,027	3,470	2,026	*60.0 cir*
Brooms	4,067	714	2,859	1,310	18.4

*No data by states

MARKETS FOR RAW MATERIALS

One of the criteria for placing certain industries in Group III is their capacity as markets of raw materials in order that industry may help balance agriculture and other primary production. While this feature of many of the industries discussed in all groups has been referred to, it is perhaps not out of place to bring together some of the data on this point for comparison. The census item "value of product" includes cost of materials, supplies, fuel, purchased energy and value added by manufacture. The chief item is raw materials. The difference between value of product and value added by manufacture is, therefore, a rough measure of the industry as a user of, and market for, materials. To be sure this is an oversimplification because such factors as the kind of process, the stage to which automatic machinery has been adapted, and the cheapness or costliness of the material itself all greatly affect the value of product handled per wage earner. By and large however, this measure is suggestive.

There are 78 industries in the United States in which the value of product is over $10,000 per wage earner. Ten of the industries are very small, employing less than a thousand wage earners each. Sixteen more are unlikely industries for the Southeast for a variety of reasons: lack of raw materials; the nature of the industry makes it concentrate in metropolitan and style centers; monopolistic industries, often covered by patents, which have become closely localized and have every reason for, and advantage in expanding in their present locations. Six of these: rice cleaning and polishing, turpentine and rosin, cottonseed oil, cigarettes, and chewing and smoking tobacco, tanning materials, are already mainly located in the Southeast. Of the 46 remaining it is striking to note how many are among the industries suggested in this study as desirable for expansion and for stimulation in the Southeast. Most are industries for which the region has, or could produce, the raw materials; most require chiefly semiskilled and unskilled labor. Some would require the importation of technical skill in order to get started. They are, in general, high wage industries, have a high value added by manufacture and after deduction of wages and salaries show an adequate balance for interest on the necessary capital. Other factors can be found for all of these in the tables in Chapter VI.

The accompanying table shows a few selected factors of these 46 industries. Following these the table includes the value of products of a group of industries important in the region. They are all low wage industries. The value of product is often less than the value added by manufacture of the first group. Their value added by manufacture is actually often less than the wages in the first group.

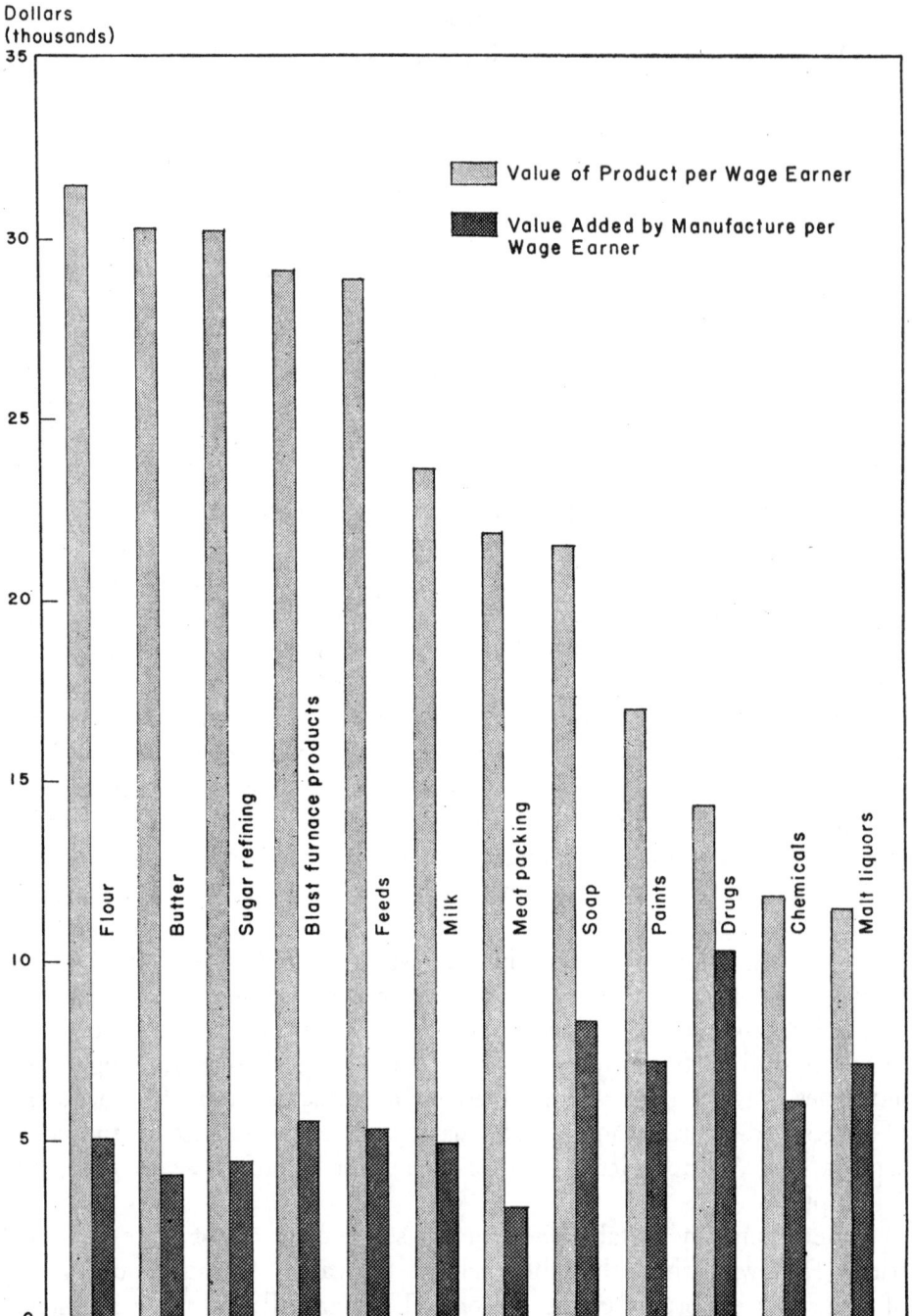

HIGH INDEX INDUSTRIES THE SOUTHEAST NEEDS

High value of product — Great markets for raw materials — High value added by manufacture — High wages and good margin for interest, profits, taxes, etc.

MANUFACTURING FOR REGIONAL BALANCE 67

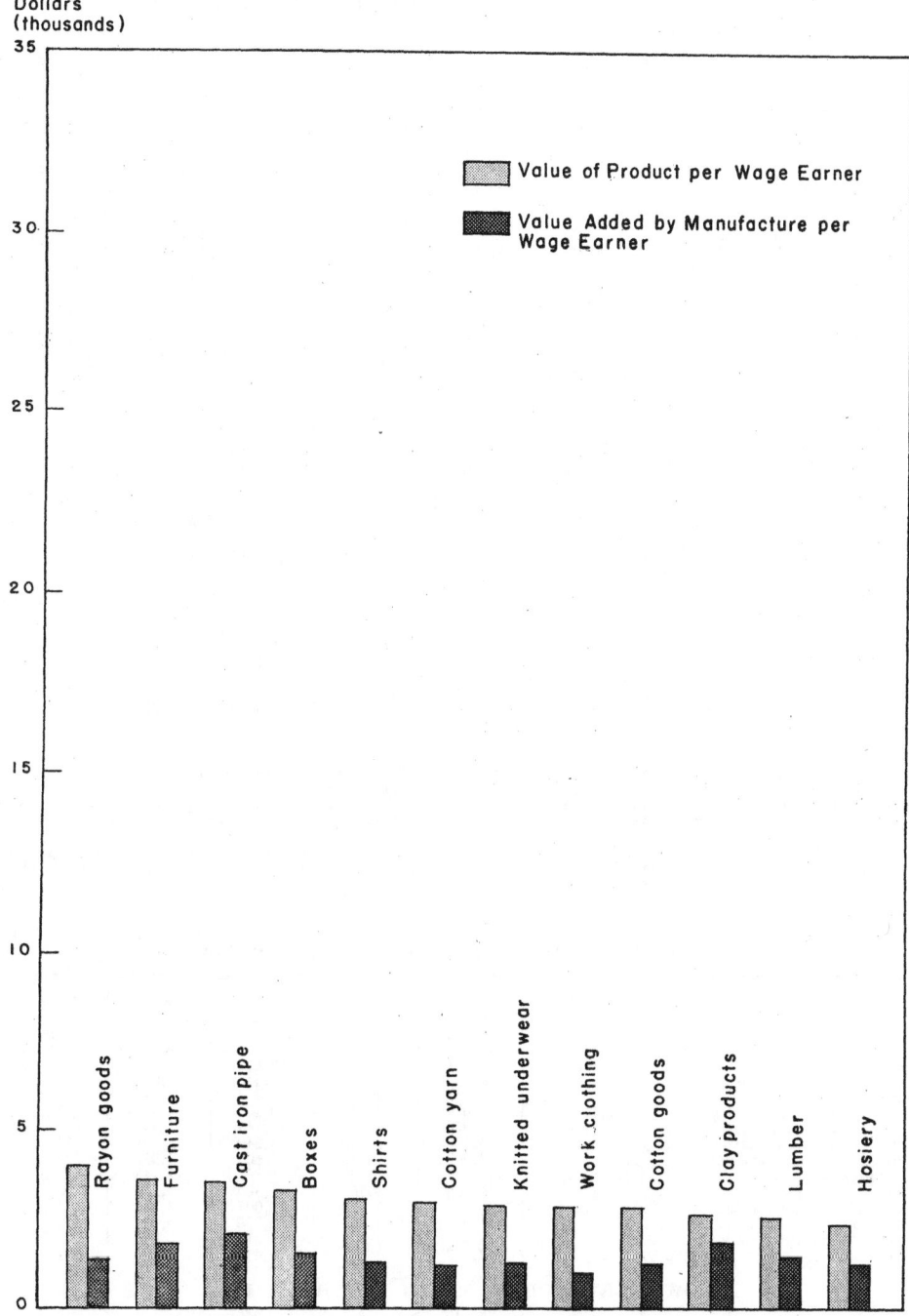

LOW INDEX INDUSTRIES THE SOUTHEAST HAS

Low value of product — Small markets for raw materials — Low value added by manufacture — Low wages and small margin for interest, profits, taxes, etc.

SOUTHERN INDUSTRY

MANUFACTURING FOR REGIONAL BALANCE—

Industries	Percent wage earners in Southeast	Number of wage earners U.S.	Number of wage earners S.E.	Wages per wage earner U.S.	Wages per wage earner S.E.	Value of product per wage earner U.S.	Value of product per wage earner S.E.	Value added by mfr. per wage earner U.S.	Value added by mfr. per wage earner S.E.
Bread and other bakery products..	9.2	239,388	22,116	1,225	955	5,975	5,300	2,922	2,530
Butter..........................	4.8	19,437	927	1,009	820	30,342	24,277	4,100	4,206
Cheese.........................	5.8	4,482	262	973	821	25,164	18,103	3,818	3,382
Evaporated and condensed milk...	*10 cir*	8,967	244T	1,110	940T	23,600	17,550T	4,930	4,230T
Corn sirup, starch, etc...........	0	7,010	......	1,490	......	19,300	......	5,610	......
Feeds (prepared for animals)......	12.5	14,397	1,804	1,100	708	28,840	19,982	5,328	3,904
Flour and other grain mill products	14.5	26,390	3,819	1,144	763	32,448	20,278	5,063	3,358
Food preparations not elsewh. clsfd.	8.6	16,794	1,450	915	582	16,592	11,584	4,634	3,084
Ice cream......................	12.8	18,664	2,391	1,140	892	15,109	11,193	7,416	5,273
Malt liquors....................	5.8	47,037	2,706	1,685	1,360	11,419	7,783	7,126	4,967
Malt............................	0	1,644	......	1,770	......	57,189	......	11,250	......
Meat packing...................	5.6	127,477	7,161	1,337	930	21,866	14,692	3,148	2,467
Poultry dressing................	*4 cir*	8,913	183T	666	536T	11,870	11,380T	2,050	1,560T
Sausage, meat pudding, etc......	*8 cir*	9,342	138G	1,220	776G	16,000	15,410G	3,240	2,515G
Carpets, wool...................	*3 cir*	30,779	*	1,045	*	5,207	*	2,554	*
Carpet yarn.....................	0	2,584	......	1,151	......	6,521	......	1,975	......
Artificial leather................	0	2,541	......	1,368	......	10,865	......	3,618	......
Asphalted-felt-base floor covering..	0	3,280	......	1,455	......	10,228	......	4,853	......
Linoleum.......................	0	4,827	......	1,368	......	7,383	......	4,218	......
Lithographing...................	*2 cir*	24,079	350K	1,492	1,172K	5,721	4,310K	3,464	2,975K
Photoengraving.................	4.5	12,364	559	2,355	1,928	6,305	5,548	5,068	4,397
Grease and tallow...............	*2 cir*	5,200	79V	1,301	856V	10,052	8,645V	3,709	3,000V
Soap............................	*2 cir*	14,008	*	1,362	*	21,508	*	8,290	*
Linseed oil......................	0	2,628	......	1,367	......	34,382	......	6,041	......
Leather, tanned and curried......	*5 cir*	48,132	1,133NC	1,212	800NC	8,059	1,08INC	2,258	2,570NC
Boots and shoes.................	*5 cir*	215,438	4,464T	888	840T	3,566	4,675T	1,634	2,250T
Pottery and porcelain (including bathroom fixtures).............	*3 cir*	33,060	678T	1,159	*	2,865	*	2,071	*
Bolts and nuts not made in rolling mills....................	*1 cir*	16,840	*	1,312	*	5,824	*	3,191	*
Forgings not made in rolling mills.	*1 cir*	18,255	*	1,515	*	6,729	*	3,265	*
Wire (from purchased rods)......	0	24,580	......	1,382	......	7,329	......	3,327	......
Wire work not elsewhere classified.	*1 cir*	33,471	224T	1,171	597T	4,915	2,653T	2,576	1,222T

*No data.
Key to abbreviations: G, Georgia; K, Kentucky; NC, North Carolina; T, Tennessee; V, Virginia. The state with the largest number of wage earners is used as a sample of the Southeast when regional data are unavailable.
  The indices for the industries in which the Southeast showed manufacture for regional balance are recapitulated here for convenience in reference. Columnar arrangement makes it possible to compare any one item of all industries better than can be done with the individual industry tables in the text.
  The contrasts between the industries of this group and those of Group I are even more striking than between groups I and II.
  Considering first the indices for the United States, it will be observed that in wages per wage earner there are only 4 below $1,000,

* * * * *

HIGH INDEX INDUSTRIES THE SOUTHEAST NEEDS

	Number wage earners	Wages per wage earner	Value of product per wage earner	Value added by mfr. per wage earner	Percent wage earners in Southeast
Shortenings, vegetable.............	4,901	$ 1,150	$48,862	$ 7,160	*15 cir*
Flour, grain mill products..........	26,390	1,144	32,448	5,063	14.5
Butter............................	19,437	1,009	30,342	4,110	4.8
Sugar refining....................	14,024	1,140	30,200	4,410	*27 cir*
Blast-furnace products............	23,075	1,647	29,145	5,532	*10 cir*
Feeds, prepared, for animals.......	14,397	1,100	28,840	5,328	12.5
Milk, evaporated, condensed.......	8,967	1,110	23,600	4,930	*10 cir*
Meat packing....................	127,477	1,337	21,866	3,148	5.6
Soap.............................	14,008	1,362	21,509	8,290	*2 cir*
Paints, pigments, varnishes........	31,664	1,350	17,005	7,149	4.7
Drugs and medicines.............	24,095	1,084	14,356	10,255	5.5
Chemicals (industrial, etc.)........	78,951	1,485	11,814	6,050	9.7
Malt liquors......................	47,037	1,685	11,419	7,126	5.8

LOW INDEX INDUSTRIES THE SOUTHEAST HAS

	Number wage earners	Wages per wage earner	Value of product per wage earner	Value added by mfr. per wage earner	Percent wage earners in Southeast
Rayon woven goods..............	57,949	845	3,965	1,391	36.0
Furniture, household..............	130,765	947	3,614	1,855	22.7
Cast iron pipe....................	17,613	1,027	3,470	2,026	*60 cir*
Boxes, wooden, except cigar.......	25,981	752	3,323	1,574	39.6
Men's shirts, except work..........	55,570	629	3,149	1,298	*13 cir*
Cotton yarn and thread...........	86,206	659	3,023	1,224	78.5
Knitted underwear...............	39,923	715	2,950	1,361	33.3
Men's work clothing..............	69,502	594	2,941	1,029	35.3
Cotton goods over 12 inches.......	336,104	761	2,877	1,313	74.0
Clay products (except pottery).....	59,585	971	2,740	1,884	18.9
Lumber and timber products......	323,928	849	2,619	1,555	44.5
Hosiery..........................	150,460	906	2,403	1,340	44.2

MANUFACTURING FOR REGIONAL BALANCE

Group III Industries

Percent wages are of value added by mfr.		Salary per salaried person		Salary per wage earner		Wage earners per salaried person		Wage and salary per wage earner		Percent wages and salary are of value added by mfr.		Balance per wage earner, for interest, profits, taxes, etc.	
U.S.	S.E.	U.S.	S.E.	U.S.	S.E.	U.S.	S.E.	U.S.	S.E.	U.S.	S.E.	U.S.	S.E.
42.0	37.9	1,914	1,713	190	182	10.1	9.5	1,415	1,137	48.4	44.9	1,507	1,393
24.6	19.5	1,403	1,461	472	557	3.0	2.6	1,481	1,377	36.4	32.7	2,619	2,829
25.5	24.0	1,464	1,051	204	261	7.2	4.0	1,177	1,077	30.8	31.8	2,641	2,305
22.5	22.2T	1,852	1,895T	367	233T	5.0	8.1T	1,477	1,173T	30.0	27.9T	3,453	3,057T
26.6	....	2,740	....	440	....	6.2	....	1,930	....	34.4	....	3,680	....
20.6	18.2	1,804	1,744	600	613	3.0	2.8	1,700	1,321	32.0	33.8	3,628	2,583
22.6	22.7	2,098	1,911	525	417	4.0	4.6	1,669	1,180	32.9	35.2	3,394	2,178
19.8	18.8	2,170	2,122	453	350	4.8	6.1	1,368	932	29.5	30.2	3,266	2,152
15.4	16.9	1,911	1,839	597	697	3.2	2.6	1,737	1,589	23.4	30.2	5,679	3,684
23.6	27.4	2,510	2,090	554	474	4.5	4.4	2,239	1,834	31.4	37.0	4,887	3,133
15.7	....	4,200	....	816	....	5.1	....	2,586	....	22.9	....	8,664	....
42.4	37.8	2,084	1,992	411	348	5.1	5.7	1,748	1,278	55.5	52.0	1,400	1,189
32.5	35.4T	1,580	1,484T	219	195T	7.2	7.6T	885	721T	43.2	46.3T	1,165	839T
37.6	30.3G	2,301	1,766G	401	205G	5.7	8.6G	1,621	981G	50.0	39.1G	1,619	1,534G
41.0	*	2,184	*	163	*	13.4	*	1,208	*	47.3	*	1,346	*
58.3	....	3,398	....	189	....	17.9	....	1,340	....	67.8	....	635	....
37.8	....	2,840	....	452	....	6.3	....	1,820	....	50.4	....	1,798	....
30.0	....	2,658	....	230	....	11.5	....	1,685	....	34.7	....	3,168	....
32.4	....	2,077	....	190	....	10.9	....	1,558	....	37.0	....	2,660	....
43.1	39.4K	2,754	2,342K	663	609K	4.2	3.8K	2,155	1,781K	62.2	57.4K	1,309	1,194K
46.4	43.9	2,778	2,642	1,020	978	2.7	2.7	3,375	2,906	66.6	66.2	1,693	1,491
35.0	28.5V	2,573	3,680V	434	977V	5.9	3.8V	1,735	1,833V	46.8	61.0V	1,974	1,167V
16.4	*	2,128	*	550	*	3.9	*	1,912	*	23.1	*	6,378	*
22.6	....	2,316	....	204	....	11.4	....	1,571	....	26.0	....	4,470	....
53.7	31.2NC	2,845	2,082NC	206	143NC	13.8	14.5NC	1,418	943NC	62.8	36.7NC	840	1,627NC
54.4	37.3T	1,950	1,815T	135	91T	14.5	20.0T	1,023	931T	62.6	41.4T	611	1,319T
56.0	*	2,467	*	196	*	12.6	*	1,355	*	65.4	*	716	*
41.1	*	2,641	*	359	*	7.4	*	1,671	*	52.4	*	1,520	*
46.4	*	3,100	*	336	*	9.2	*	1,851	*	56.7	*	1,414	*
41.5	....	2,530	....	326	....	7.8	....	1,708	....	51.3	....	1,619	....
45.5	48.7T	2,577	2,315T	339	165T	7.6	14.0T	1,510	762	58.6	62.8T	1,066	460T

and 18 of the 31 are above the national average ($1,180). About half are quite high in value of product and 21 are above the national average ($7,085). Like Group II but unlike Group I, they offer considerable opportunity to technical and clerical workers, indicated by the small number of wage earners per salaried person. In balance after expenditure for wages and salary 4 of these industries are quite low but 21 are above and 11 are more than twice the national average ($1,441).

Again the part in the Southeast is lower than the whole industry but considerably better than the regional average. For the 18 industries for which data for the region or a sample state are available only 4 are below the regional average ($759). In only 3 cases is the number of wage earners per salaried person higher than the regional average (12.5) and most are below the national average (7). In 2 cases the balance after salary and wages are deducted is quite low but in all the others it is well above the regional average ($1,066) and in 11 it is above the national average ($1,441).

* * * * * *

[Notes on table at bottom of opposite page, which presents the data used in graphs on pages 66-67.]

A BALANCED ECONOMY FOR THE SOUTHEAST

should include more industries, such as the first group, which process large quantities of raw material (indicated by high value of product relative to value added by manufacture). These would supply markets for present and potential products of the region. Many also pay good wages, returns on investment and profits (the principal items in "Value added by manufacture"). Contrast with these the second group, where value of product is less than value added by manufacture in the first group, and value added is near the wages in the first group.

CHAPTER V

OPTIMUM PRODUCTION AND OPPORTUNITY

The Southeast has a wealth of agricultural and forest products and mineral resources upon which to base a varied manufacturing economy. As was pointed out in the discussion of the industries in Group I, the attention of the region has, in the main, been directed toward the first rough processing of its chief crops and resources. Only rarely have efforts been directed toward finishing them for the ultimate consumer. The sheer physical bulk of many of these materials made it good national economy to manufacture them near the source of the raw products. Most of the industries involved required relatively little capital to start a unit of satisfactory size. Lack of capital used to be a deterrent to manufacturing in the South. For really promising industries it is less so now when there is idle money in the banks and the government in the lending business. Most needed only a few highly trained technicians. In some industries, such as cotton textiles, the region gradually built up such a personnel by some importation, by long experience and with the aid of its textile schools; in others, experience and the occasional importation of technicians were sufficient.

Nearly all these industries needed large supplies of labor that was cheap, much of it unskilled. At most they required semiskilled workers who could be readily trained on the job. In quantity the labor supply has been so large that for generations the region has been exporting population. In quality, at least theoretically, its virtues have become axiomatic: Anglo-Saxon, homogeneous, intelligent, willing to learn and easy to teach, tractable, satisfied with moderate, even low, wages. These claims may have been exaggerated, but their relative truth is proved by the movement to the South of industries for which this type of labor is an important asset.

All these industries have been, and many are still, important to the Southeast for the markets they provided, the jobs they offered and the profits they made. But the markets have been for too few raw materials to encourage a varied agriculture, and the kind of products too few to create a varied trade. The 11 southeastern states in 1937 had industries falling into 241 of the 352 classifications in the *Census of Manufactures*. New

York alone had 284, Pennsylvania 283, New Jersey 273, Illinois 272. Even California had 257. The jobs in the chief southeastern industries have paid low wages, have required a relatively small variety of skills, and mainly a low level of skill. In New England, in contrast, the workers graduated from their first industry, textiles, to boot and shoe making and the metal trades, and thence to machinery manufacture. The profits of southeastern industry, often high in the early stages, have dwindled.

Indeed many of these industries, when considered potentially, are found to be either stationary or declining. The reader of Chapter II must have been struck by the fact that many industries of which the Southeast has a large share were noted as having decreased since 1925 by some or all of the measures. And so, always desirable, it has become urgent for the region to encourage and foster not only more, but more varied, industry. One of the greatest problems is the need for developing among the labor force more, and more varied, skills.

THE LACK OF SKILLS

This lack has been implicit in the statistics already given—the low indices per wage earner. It is even more apparent in a comparison of the region's share of wage earners and wages, of salaried persons and salaries, of value of product and value added by manufacture.

The fact that the Southeast has 20 percent of the wage earners in an industry does not mean that it has that proportion of the industry by any other measures. Because of the regulations regarding disclosure of operation of individual establishments, it is not possible to calculate regional totals for all industries. But it is possible to secure such figures for 55 industries ranging from turpentine and rosin, all located in the Southeast, to electrical machinery not elsewhere classified, of which only 0.5 percent is in the Southeast. The list involves, if often in small amounts, a wide variety of products, skills, markets and capital invested.

Except for the two industries entirely located in the Southeast there is not a single instance in which the region has as high a proportion of the total wage dispensed as it has of the wage earners. In 7 cases it comes within 10 percent: cottonseed oil, meal and cake, 99.9 percent; cigarettes, 99.6 percent; cotton woven goods, 95.7 percent; rayon woven goods, 94.0 percent; awnings, tents and sails, 93.8 percent; cotton yarn and thread, 92.3 percent; knitted underwear, 90.3 percent. All are low wage industries wherever they are located. In 22 cases the Southeast has at least 25 percent less of the total wages than of the wage earners. In two industries the regional share of the wages paid is very low indeed: in canned and cured fish the Southeast has 26 percent of the wage earners but paid out only 15.3 percent of the wages, or 58.8 percent of its proper

The Share of the Southeast in Fifty-five Industries

Industry	Percent in Southeast of total:						Percent other Southeastern factors are of Southeastern wage earners:				
	Wage earners	Wages	Value of product	Value added by manufacture	Salaried persons	Salaries	Wages	Value of product	Value added by manufacture	Salaried persons	Salaries
Turpentine and rosin	100.0	100.0	100.0	100.0	100.0	100.0					
Cane sugar manufacture	100.0	100.0	100.0	100.0	100.0	100.0					
Cigarettes	94.7	94.4	95.5	96.5	92.4	92.2	99.6	101.0	102.0	97.5	97.3
Cotton yarn and thread	78.5	72.6	74.4	71.1	55.0	54.8	92.3	94.6	90.5	70.0	69.9
Cotton woven goods (over 12 inches)	74.0	70.9	74.1	72.0	64.1	64.9	95.7	100.2	97.1	86.6	87.7
Cottonseed oil, cake and meal	68.0	67.9	68.7	61.3	59.7	60.7	99.9	101.1	90.2	87.8	89.3
Rice cleaning and polishing	67.0	52.0	55.8	47.4	64.3	58.8	77.5	83.2	70.7	95.9	87.8
Fertilizers	62.3	45.7	57.2	52.7	60.5	55.4	73.4	91.7	84.6	97.1	89.0
Sumber and timber products	44.5	27.9	33.1	32.2	40.9	38.5	62.6	74.4	72.4	92.1	86.4
Hosiery	44.2	34.8	39.3	36.6	33.1	34.3	78.6	89.0	82.7	74.8	77.5
Boxes, wooden (not cigar)	39.6	26.3	25.4	26.6	23.6	24.3	66.4	64.1	67.1	59.6	61.2
Rayon broad woven goods	36.0	33.8	34.6	33.1	24.3	22.4	94.0	96.0	91.7	67.4	62.2
Men's and boys' work clothing	35.3	28.6	31.8	27.0	24.0	22.4	81.0	90.2	76.5	68.1	63.5
Distilled liquors	34.1	28.0	36.0	32.0	35.6	35.7	82.1	105.8	93.7	104.5	104.5
Knitted underwear	33.3	30.1	30.0	28.8	20.7	21.7	90.3	90.2	86.5	62.2	65.2
Beverages, nonalcoholic	30.4	27.1	32.2	31.7	27.5	31.5	89.1	106.0	104.5	90.5	103.5
Planing mill products	28.2	19.5	23.2	20.7	20.9	19.1	69.1	82.2	73.4	74.1	67.7
Wood, turned and shaped	27.4	23.0	24.2	22.0	20.7	20.5	84.0	88.4	80.3	75.5	74.7
Ice, manufactured	26.4	19.9	22.8	22.4	30.0	25.4	75.5	86.4	85.0	113.6	96.2
Canned and cured fish, etc	26.0	15.3	13.0	14.4	16.9	12.3	58.8	50.0	55.4	65.1	47.3
Furniture (household and office)	22.7	17.0	18.0	16.6	14.0	14.7	74.8	79.4	73.0	61.7	64.7
Marble, etc., cut and shaped	22.5	16.9	16.4	17.5	17.5	16.0	75.0	73.0	77.8	77.8	71.2
Bone black, carbon black	19.3	16.5	14.1	12.8	8.7	10.3	85.6	73.0	66.4	45.0	53.3
Clay products (other than pottery)	18.9	13.3	14.9	14.1	15.1	16.4	70.4	78.7	74.5	80.0	86.7
Brooms	18.4	13.5	13.6	14.0	16.8	13.4	73.4	73.6	76.2	91.3	72.8
Mattress and bedsprings	14.6	11.0	12.0	11.8	12.3	14.4	75.2	82.1	80.8	84.2	98.6
Flour, other grain mill products	14.5	9.7	9.0	9.6	12.7	11.5	66.8	62.1	66.2	87.5	79.2
Coffins, caskets, etc	13.7	9.9	10.2	8.5	11.0	10.6	72.2	74.4	62.0	80.2	77.3
Concrete products	13.5	9.9	9.7	9.4	12.4	11.9	73.2	71.9	69.6	91.8	88.1
Ice cream	12.8	10.0	9.5	9.1	15.5	14.9	78.0	74.2	71.1	121.1	116.3
Feeds, prepared, for animals	12.5	8.1	8.7	9.2	13.3	12.8	65.0	69.6	73.6	106.3	102.5
Canned and dried fruits, pickles, etc	11.3	6.0	5.7	5.6	7.6	5.8	53.2	50.5	49.6	67.3	51.4
Heating and cooking apparatus (not elec.)	9.7	6.7	5.4	5.2	4.1	4.4	69.0	55.6	53.6	42.3	45.4
Chemicals not elsewhere classified	9.7	7.7	9.7	10.3	7.3	6.5	79.4	100.0	106.2	75.4	67.0
Structural and ornamental steel	9.6	7.7	8.1	8.1	10.1	9.9	80.3	84.5	84.5	105.2	103.2
Bread and other bakery products	9.2	7.2	8.2	8.0	9.9	8.9	78.3	89.1	87.0	107.5	96.9
Newspaper and periodical publishing	8.9	7.3	6.4	6.8	8.9	7.2	82.0	72.0	76.4	100.0	80.8
Miscellaneous food preparations	8.6	5.5	6.0	5.7	6.8	6.7	64.0	70.0	66.3	79.0	77.8
Confectionery	8.4	6.4	7.7	7.6	10.2	9.3	76.1	91.5	90.5	121.2	110.9
Awnings, tents, sails, etc	8.0	7.5	6.9	7.7	8.9	8.7	93.8	86.2	96.1	111.1	108.9
Book and job printing	6.2	5.1	4.9	4.7	5.4	4.7	82.0	79.0	75.8	87.1	75.8
Cheese	5.8	4.9	4.2	5.2	10.4	7.5	84.5	72.4	89.6	179.5	129.4
Malt liquors	5.8	4.6	3.9	4.0	5.9	4.9	79.2	67.2	69.0	101.7	84.5
Meat packing	5.6	3.9	3.8	4.4	5.0	4.8	69.7	67.9	78.5	89.3	85.6
Sheet metal work	5.6	4.2	5.5	4.9	5.5	4.7	75.0	98.3	87.5	98.3	84.0
Drugs and medicines	5.5	3.7	4.8	4.5	7.2	6.2	67.4	87.3	81.8	131.0	112.9
Butter	4.8	3.9	3.8	4.9	5.4	5.6	81.1	79.0	102.0	112.5	116.6
Paints, pigment, and varnish	4.7	3.7	4.0	4.1	5.1	5.7	78.7	85.0	87.2	108.5	121.2
Photoengraving	4.5	3.7	4.0	3.9	4.6	4.3	82.2	88.7	86.5	102.0	95.6
Textile machinery and parts	4.5	3.3	4.1	3.6	3.7	3.6	73.3	91.0	80.0	82.2	80.0
Liquors, rectified and blended	4.1	3.5	3.8	4.0	4.8	4.6	85.4	92.6	97.5	117.1	112.2
Machinery not elsewhere classified	4.1	2.9	3.3	3.1	3.3	3.0	70.6	80.5	75.6	80.4	73.2
Foundry products	4.0	2.9	3.7	3.5	5.9	4.9	72.4	92.4	87.5	147.8	122.4
Machine shop products	3.3	2.6	2.5	2.8	3.0	2.6	78.8	75.6	84.8	91.0	78.7
Electrical machinery	0.5	0.4	0.6	0.4	0.4	0.4	80.0	120.0	80.0	80.0	80.0

proportion; in canned and dried fruits, vegetables, etc. the region has 11.3 percent of the wage earners and paid out only 6 percent of the wages, or 53.2 percent of its proper proportion.

All this is belaboring the well-known fact that southeastern wage

OPTIMUM PRODUCTION AND OPPORTUNITY

scales are the lowest in the nation. Taken with the value of product and the value added by manufacture, the figures underline still another point: that the Southeast has the cheaper, less skilled parts of the individual industries. For example, in 46 of the 55 industries the region's proportion of the total value of product is less than its percent of the wage earners, and in 49 of the 55 the same is true of value added by manufacture. In 18 cases the value of product, and in 18 cases the value added by manufacture the discrepancy as compared with wage earners is 25 percent or more, and in one or two cases is nearly 50 percent.

All this might indicate that southeastern manufacturers value and sell their products more cheaply than those of other regions. This may be true in such industries, for example, as lumber and timber products, wooden boxes, concrete products, ice cream, or newspapers which are sold chiefly in a local low price market. But it would hardly seem necessary in the case of canned fish, marble and stone, brooms, floor, coffins, canned fruit and vegetables, to name a few where the discrepancies are largest. If manufacturers in the region are willing and able to do this they should have no difficulty in competing in the national markets.

But this undoubtedly is only part of the story. Any layman knows that in many industries the Southeast actually does manufacture the cheaper kinds of products going to make up an industry classification: a larger part of the children's and men's cotton hose lowers the value of the region's share in hosiery; a larger share of the cheap berry tills, peach baskets, and vegetable hampers in which to ship the truck products of its long growing season, rather than the substantial boxes for shipping the machinery and appliances for the Northeast and Middle West, make for a lower share in the value of wooden boxes; its furniture, coffins, and stoves are actually cheaper products; its share of canned fruits and vegetables is weighted with tomatoes and pickles rather than with fancy peas and asparagus; its share of the textile machinery and parts industry consists mainly of the "parts."

In a few industries this is not true. In cigarettes, nonalcoholic beverages, and chemicals the region's share of both value of product and value added by manufacture is higher than its share of the wage earners. The first two are consumers' goods with patents and trademarks owned by parent companies in the region. The third is so new an industry in the Southeast that the region's resources which attracted the factories and newest equipment and processes give it an advantage. In cotton goods and distilled liquors the percent of the value of product is slightly higher than that of the wage earners: the region has spent half a century learning the skills in the first; Kentucky has spent longer building a reputation in the other.

THE DEVELOPMENT OF SKILLS

These few exceptions and the quite understandable reasons for them make all the more impressive the persistently lower percentages in practically all industries. The reasons are complex; lack of capital, markets, skills, and one of the greatest is surely skills. Skills of all kind, even of the "unskilled."[1] This group makes up 20 percent of the workers in all manufacturing industry. For the laborers in brick and tile factories, 64.4 percent of the personnel, do different work from that of the laborers in sawmills, 58.3 percent of the personnel. The facility, deftness and speed of the "semiskilled." This is the great machine operative class, and constitutes some 40 percent of all workers in manufacturing industry, the proportions ranging from 9.3 percent in fertilizer factories to 81 percent in cotton garment making. A few days, a few weeks, or at most a few months suffice to train these laborers, helpers and operatives; but as industry and education are at present constituted in the United States they must be trained on the job.

More important is the skill of the artisans, journeymen and craftsmen; of the mechanics who keep the machines in order; of the foremen who keep the work flowing and the workers working smoothly. These groups make up some 22 percent of the workers in all manufacturing industry and range from 2 or 3 percent in cotton garment factories to 36.8 percent in furniture and 45.4 percent in marble and stone cutting. To train these workers takes years instead of months. They, too, must learn on the job. Specific training in schools or courses or by solitary study can shorten the process, but all these methods are empty without long experience in the realities of production. These workers must learn on the job to master the infinite variations of machines and materials, of situations and of men. Specialized industry must train such workers for its many specialisms. The community, the state or the region which has none of a given industry can expect none of its group of specialists. A few can be brought from some established center to start a few wheels in a new locality, and the very keeping of those wheels turning will produce the skill and experience for an expansion of the industry.

The most important skills in modern manufacturing are those of the engineers and technicians who plan the work; who test and improve the product, the processes and the machinery; who find new uses for the raw materials and the finished goods. Some of these functions are still carried on by the skilled workmen and foremen, by proprietors and managers. But many industries are placing less reliance on rule of thumb and on fortuitous inspiration. They need precision in the processes and trained imagination for invention. And so the professional group is growing: it

---

[1] See accompanying table.

OPTIMUM PRODUCTION AND OPPORTUNITY

PERCENT DISTRIBUTION, BY SOCIAL-ECONOMIC GROUPS, OF THE GAINFUL WORKERS BY INDUSTRIES

Industry	Total gainful workers	Professional persons	Proprietors, managers, officials	Clerks and kindred workers	Skilled workers and foremen	Semi-skilled workers	Un-skilled workers	Total semi-skilled and unskilled
FOOD AND KINDRED PRODUCTS		Percent	Percent	Percent	Percent	Percent	Percent	Percent
Bakeries	281,885	0.1	7.5	14.8	2.8	69.2	5.6	74.8
Butter, cheese, condensed milk	88,900	0.8	12.3	19.3	6.4	38.9	22.4	61.3
Candy	71,294	0.2	5.7	16.0	4.7	64.4	9.0	73.4
Fish curing and packing	16,288	0.1	4.9	5.9	6.7	43.7	38.7	82.4
Flour and grain mills	67,233	0.8	9.3	18.4	30.0	16.3	25.1	41.4
Liquor and beverages	50,403	0.6	16.5	19.8	6.7	37.1	19.2	56.3
Fruit and vegetable canning	56,235	0.4	7.0	10.7	9.9	36.0	35.9	71.9
Slaughter and packing houses	164,882	0.5	3.9	22.5	8.1	37.2	27.9	65.1
Sugar factories and refineries	23,503	3.2	3.7	14.1	17.7	19.9	41.4	61.3
Other food factories	86,630	1.2	11.1	22.1	8.0	36.5	21.1	57.6
TEXTILES AND THEIR PRODUCTS								
A. TEXTILE MILL PRODUCTS								
Carpet mills	44,499	1.5	1.9	8.9	8.8	67.2	11.7	78.9
Cordage and rope	11,869	0.5	3.5	11.3	10.5	48.5	25.8	74.3
Jute, hemp, linen mills	8,015	0.8	5.2	13.2	9.2	58.6	13.2	71.8
Cotton mills	422,204	0.2	0.9	2.8	8.2	73.8	14.1	87.9
Knitting mills	174,912	0.2	2.3	7.2	6.0	78.4	5.9	84.3
Lace and embroidery mills	16,336	3.6	7.8	8.9	4.4	71.4	3.9	75.3
Silk mills	171,140	0.4	2.0	7.3	7.1	76.0	7.2	83.2
Textile dyeing, finishing, printing	47,023	1.2	2.1	9.6	10.4	58.9	17.7	76.6
Woolen and worsted mills	144,513	0.4	1.8	6.4	7.7	73.1	10.6	83.7
Other and not specified textile mills	134,607	1.9	4.7	12.0	9.4	61.2	10.7	71.9
B. THE CUTTING-UP INDUSTRIES								
Shirt, collar, cuff	68,776	0.1	2.4	6.6	3.4	81.1	6.4	87.5
Suit, coat, overall	313,138	0.5	4.8	3.5	54.9	34.8	1.5	36.3
Glove	22,896		3.3	6.7	3.3	81.3	5.4	86.7
Hats (felt)	34,770	0.8	4.5	9.6	3.8	77.2	4.2	81.4
Corset	15,308	1.0	4.0	16.7	3.6	71.8	2.8	74.6
Awning, sail, and tent	8,311	0.2	16.4	14.5	6.6	53.2	9.1	62.3
Other clothing factories	334,958	1.9	4.9	8.1	2.1	81.2	1.8	83.0
FOREST PRODUCTS								
Furniture	268,098	0.6	3.8	8.7	36.8	34.3	15.8	50.1
Saw and planing mills	454,503	0.3	4.5	3.5	15.9	17.6	58.3	75.9
Other woodworking	122,274	0.5	5.2	5.8	21.5	32.1	34.9	67.0
PAPER AND ALLIED PRODUCTS								
Paper and pulp mills	179,792	1.2	3.0	11.6	14.3	38.3	31.6	69.9
Paper box	24,656	0.3	7.3	11.1	9.9	60.1	11.4	71.5
PRINTING, PUBLISHING AND ALLIED INDUSTRIES								
Blank book, envelope, tag, paper bag	38,941	1.0	5.9	21.3	14.8	45.8	11.1	56.9
Printing, publishing, engraving	544,606	0.6	8.1	27.2	44.9	16.4	2.9	19.3
CHEMICALS AND ALLIED PRODUCTS								
Charcoal and coke works	11,766	3.0	2.2	8.8	19.7	17.2	49.0	66.2
Explosives, ammunitions, fireworks	19,404	3.7	3.2	14.9	16.7	33.9	27.7	61.6
Fertilizer	28,169	0.7	4.9	12.9	6.3	9.3	65.8	75.1
Paint and varnish	37,074	3.9	9.7	32.1	8.1	28.1	18.1	46.2
Rayon	33,982	2.3	0.8	5.4	12.8	63.4	15.4	78.8
Soap	22,983	2.7	6.0	30.5	11.8	26.1	22.9	49.0
Other chemical factories	179,880	7.7	7.6	26.2	12.7	22.5	23.3	45.8
PRODUCTS OF PETROLEUM AND COAL								
Petroleum refineries	173,798	3.8	4.5	21.0	23.8	20.3	26.6	46.9
RUBBER PRODUCTS								
Rubber	166,391	1.5	3.1	16.2	10.2	50.3	18.7	69.0
LEATHER AND ITS MANUFACTURES								
Tanneries	58,420	0.6	2.9	7.4	6.8	52.0	30.3	82.3
Leather belt, leather goods, etc.	26,634	0.7	7.2	15.4	5.3	63.6	7.7	71.3
Shoe	271,451	0.3	1.8	8.0	4.5	78.0	7.5	85.5
Harness and saddle	9,103	0.1	6.7	4.5	3.3	79.7	5.8	85.5
Trunk, suitcase and bag	8,461	0.3	5.9	12.1	8.1	61.0	12.5	73.5
STONE, CLAY AND GLASS PRODUCTS								
Cement, lime, artificial stone	83,636	2.2	6.1	9.3	15.3	18.7	48.4	67.1
Brick, tile, and terra-cotta	97,245	0.7	4.6	5.7	8.3	16.3	64.4	80.7
Potteries	42,921	1.0	3.3	7.1	6.2	55.7	26.7	82.4
Glass	97,729	0.9	3.1	9.0	13.2	44.0	29.8	73.8
Marble and stone yards	50,430	2.6	7.7	9.1	45.4	18.7	16.5	35.2
IRON AND STEEL AND THEIR PRODUCTS—NOT INCLUDING MACHINERY								
Blast furnaces and steel rolling	620,894	2.0	1.7	9.3	25.2	19.5	42.3	61.8
Not specified metal industries	168,899	1.2	3.0	6.6	35.1	21.9	32.2	54.1

Industry	Total gainful workers	Professional persons	Proprietors, managers, officials	Clerks and kindred workers	Skilled workers and foremen	Semi-skilled workers	Un-skilled workers	Total semi-skilled and un-skilled
		Percent	Percent	Percent	Percent	Percent	Percent	Percent
NONFERROUS METALS AND THEIR PRODUCTS								
Brass mills	69,964	1.5	3.6	12.2	29.9	29.9	22.9	52.8
Clock and watch	25,096	0.9	2.6	11.9	13.4	64.4	6.9	71.3
Copper	21,199	3.0	1.9	8.5	26.0	17.5	43.1	60.6
Gold and silver	19,326	1.5	3.6	15.1	25.6	46.4	7.8	54.2
Jewelry	39,458	1.1	6.0	14.8	32.0	44.6	1.6	46.2
Lead and zinc	18,615	2.8	2.6	9.7	17.4	13.5	54.0	67.5
Tinware, enamelware, etc.	97,415	1.1	5.3	10.6	32.1	28.7	22.1	50.8
Other metal factories	41,903	2.5	4.6	13.6	17.2	41.3	20.9	62.2
MACHINERY—NOT INCLUDING TRANSPORTATION EQUIPMENT								
Agricultural implement	53,244	1.5	3.9	21.2	30.6	21.2	21.6	42.8
Electrical machinery and supply	383,570	5.2	3.5	22.2	24.8	33.8	10.4	44.2
Other iron and steel machinery	1,213,548	2.6	4.0	12.8	39.9	25.4	15.3	40.7
TRANSPORTATION EQUIPMENT— AIR, LAND, AND WATER								
Automobile	640,474	1.6	1.9	10.3	31.9	34.1	20.3	54.4
Wagon and carriage	9,144	0.4	6.2	7.3	29.5	39.9	16.6	56.5
Ship and boat building	93,437	2.0	1.7	5.5	44.7	26.8	19.4	46.2
MISCELLANEOUS INDUSTRIES								
Broom and brush	18,873	0.2	9.3	19.1	5.3	51.9	14.2	66.1
Button	11,340	0.2	4.0	8.2	8.8	68.2	10.5	78.7
Piano and organ	18,151	0.6	4.8	11.8	21.7	50.3	10.9	61.2
Straw	2,290	0.3	2.0	4.5	5.1	80.8	7.4	88.2
Cigar and tobacco	149,563	0.1	3.1	8.0	4.1	70.3	14.3	84.6
Other miscellaneous manufacturing indust.	360,023	1.6	8.7	16.5	13.0	40.5	19.8	60.3
Other nonspecified manufacturing industries	465,559	1.4	3.4	13.5	20.8	33.9	26.9	60.8
TOTAL	10,474,860	1.5	4.3	12.3	22.0	39.8	20.1	59.9

Source: Alba M. Edwards, *A Social-Economic Grouping of the Gainful Workers of the United States* (based on 1930 census). United States Department of Commerce. Government Printing Office, 1938.

makes up some 1.5 percent of all workers attached to manufacturing. The range is great, from 0.1 percent in shirt factories and fish curing and packing to 7.7 percent in chemicals. They learn their methods in technical schools, but like the others, they must learn effectiveness in the production process. They often graduate into the management class.

And so the reasons for the lack of skills in the Southeast boil down to lack of manufacturing in which to learn and practice skills. The way to have them in the Southeast is to build up varied industries. Some of the professional group and of the skilled workers and foremen may have to be imported. That was done occasionally in textiles, the region's oldest industry, one needing few in these brackets. It is being done in chemicals, the region's newest industry, one requiring many and highly trained experts. The planning board or the chamber of commerce seeking a new industry could be as helpful to the potential entrepreneur in supplying sources for these skills as these agencies now are in finding sites or subsidies or sources of capital. Else, like a projected little broom factory that would have been a boon to its community in the North Carolina mountains, the new venture may fail for lack of one man, or never get started at all.

OPTIMUM PRODUCTION AND OPPORTUNITY

OPPORTUNITY AND THE REGION'S YOUTH

But the region does not have to depend entirely upon importation. It has schools of engineering and of business administration which train young men in a variety of technical skills, and could train them in more if there was any demand. As it is, the cream of each class is skimmed off to go to industrial laboratories, engineering departments and managerial apprenticeships in other regions. The Southeast is losing much of its potential industrial leadership just as for a century it has lost some of its most virile people. For optimum production and optimum living it needs varied opportunity for youth as much as it needs varied manufacturing and agriculture.

Below the professional and technical level the region can help itself by vocational education. The states of the Old South were late in developing schools. They are proud of their progress and can be excused for being late to realize that the goal for every boy or girl is not the liberal arts college, nor college preparation nor even high school. In the preoccupation with this theoretical ideal the more expensive, slightly despised vocational education has been neglected. In a town where practically all the jobs and the opportunity for advancement lie in textiles the students solve problems in papering walls without learning there is such a thing as mill arithmetic. In a town where the opportunities for work lie in furniture factories the students learn a smattering of French but not the difference between woods.

A few school authorities and a few industrial managers have awakened to this situation. They have established cooperative schemes by which students may learn something of the dominant industry—the qualities and processing of its raw materials, the design and uses of its products. These students receive credit for work on a variety of actual production machines set apart in a training department of the plant. But it takes farsighted leaders to make so drastic a break with tradition. The schoolman must give up the popular delusion that all his students are going to have far better jobs than those the community affords. The industrialist must be willing to risk criticism that he is using public funds to train his future workers.

It is possible that recent federal legislation may indirectly stimulate such cooperation. The wage hour law limits the period in which learners may be paid less than the standard minimum wage. This period is rarely long enough for the totally inexperienced worker to acquire sufficient proficiency to "make out." The young person who "knows a hawk from a handsaw," who has had some experience with the machines, some feel of the process, avoids the first stumbling days and weeks; he has an advantage over his fellows in getting a job and considerable advantage in learning it within the prescribed time. During the depression, manufacturing companies had little need to train young workers; they could not employ all the experienced adults. Now they train no more than absolutely necessary because of the rules about learners. The country has been warned that it has a shortage of skilled workers in such lines as tool making for the defense program. When production on a large scale reaches the machine stage the country may find that it has a shortage of machine operatives.

There is one field in which the schools, even those in the Southeast, have considered it proper to give vocational education, namely in clerical work. If the public is willing to have its money spent to teach young people stenography and typing for work in factory offices, it is difficult to see why the same public cannot be convinced that it is just as proper to train young people for the vastly more numerous jobs in the factory itself. In the industries of Group I, the big industries of the Southeast, there are 10 or 20 or even 40 wage earners per salaried person. But clerical work, office work, is more desired because it is more respectable—one can wear a white collar. And many young people in the Southeast will still prefer it to jobs, often more lucrative, in the factory just as their contemporaries do in other regions. That is another reason for the encouragement of industries in Group II and Group III. In these the salaried workers are two or three times as numerous as in those of Group I.

The relative opportunities for white collar workers in different industries are even more clearly shown in the table pp. 75-76. "Clerks and kindred workers" are given separately from the professional and managerial workers; the industry classifications used, while not exactly the same, are roughly parallel. In cotton mills, clerical and kindred workers constitute 2.8 percent of all persons attached to the industry; in saw and planing mills, 3.5 percent; brick and tile factories, 5.7 percent; shirts, etc., 6.6 percent; and in other clothing factories similar percentages; knitting mills, 7.2 percent; tobacco manufacturing, 8.0 percent. These are among the largest industries in the Southeast, the industries of Group I. Corresponding figures for clerical workers in some of Group II and III are as follows: paper and pulp, 11.6 percent; sail, awning, and tent, 14.5 percent; bakeries, 14.8 percent; flour mills, 18.4 percent; butter, cheese, etc., 19.3 percent; packing houses, 22.5 percent; "other chemicals," 26.2 percent; printing, publishing, and engraving, 27.2 percent; paint and varnish, 32.1 percent. The industries that will help to balance agricultural economy and vary the manufacturing base also will offer more opportunities for employment in the white collar class.

THE NATIONAL EMERGENCY AND REGIONAL OPPORTUNITY

Now no picture or planning prospect of southern industry at this time could fail to envisage the national emergency and regional opportunity for development. That the Southeast has long needed this balance, this variety and these opportunities can scarcely be doubted. In so far as the defense program offers the region a chance to hasten the process, it can be utilized in both hastening and strengthening regional strategy for a better balanced economy in harmony with optimum programs for the region and for the nation. Yet, to a very large extent the government must go for its most pressing needs to the plants which are already prepared with equipment and skills to produce them. Most of these plants are in other regions than the Southeast. This, then, is a difficult problem for the region. In so far as the South neglects its opportunities here, it not only fails to develop and use its own resources, but is recreant to the trust of giving work to its people.

It is assumed that its textiles will receive large orders, but since most of the branches of these industries are overdeveloped, like agriculture, they may need little expansion. Of more immediate need is the task of expanding its chemical, iron and steel and shipbuilding industries for the threefold objectives of meeting emergency needs, of developing new skills and capacity in the South, and of aiding the region in holding to the gains when the emergency relaxes. Its pulp and paper industries will surely grow because of the international situation and of new technological gains. To retain these gains when competition from trade-hungry nations is resumed will constitute an important "defense" on the new frontier.

The greatest opportunity for the region lies in the chance to begin manufacturing for itself. The pleadings of southern governors and the efforts of all the boosters represent just one phase, and a really minor effort. We may be sure that most of the defense orders may go to other regions. Other governors are just as eager for the new plants to be located in their states. Other agencies with better priority schedules are working even harder, which is logical and normal. Likewise, we must remember that an overbalance of employment on these orders and preoccupation with the new industries may slow their expansion in manufacture for normal peacetime consumption.

Since this aspect of the regional problem will be treated more at length in a forthcoming volume on the Structure of Southern Industry by Milton S. Heath, it is needed only to point up its role and implications here. In the meantime, the Southeast may now have a chance at manufacturing for its own markets, a chance to build the industries of Group II and III. Most of these are growing anyhow; the region should take this opportunity to build some of the normal expansion and of the specially stimulated growth of this period. If it can learn to manufacture for itself and for some measure of regional balance, the Southeast will have used the emergency for a good purpose, for an approach toward optimum production.

This is not a proposal for this region to grab the industries when other areas are not looking, but a suggestion that it seize the opportunity to do what it should have done long ago. Other parts of the country have complained bitterly at federal expenditure in the South during the depression. They can hardly complain if these states learn to help themselves. If the Southeast can and will balance its own economy it will solve one national problem. And "out of this nettle, danger, we pluck this flower, safety"—safety from a possible enemy, and regional-national welfare for the future.

CHAPTER VI

THE STATISTICAL PICTURE

There are many industries in the United States besides the 116 which have been discussed as located mainly in the Southeast or as possible and desirable for the region. Many for obvious reasons, others for reasons suggested in Chapter V, are impracticable for development in the region. The tables at the end of this chapter show all the manufacturing industries in the United States. Those which have been discussed are included in their group setting for comparative purposes. There are 55 industries for which the data of the census permits calculation of regional figures. For these the southeastern indices are given in bold-faced type.

A few comments on these tables are, perhaps, in order. For convenience in reference they follow as closely as possible the arrangement of data in the tables presented in earlier chapters. In all cases the number of wage earners is given first, in order to convey an idea of the industry's relative size and importance. The second column gives the actual percent of the wage earners found in the 11 southeastern states. In the majority of industries, however, the actual percent in the Southeast cannot be ascertained because of regulations forbidding disclosure of plant operations when a state has few establishments. The census does, however, report the number of wage earners for many states for which it does not give the other data separately. Therefore, it has been possible to estimate with some degree of accuracy the number, and hence the proportion in the Southeast. In some cases where many states have a single establishment and there was no other guide, the wage earners for all known states were subtracted from the total of "other states," the remainder averaged over the remaining number of plants and the Southeast allowed its pro rata share on a basis of establishments. The doubtful industries were then checked by persons having a combined knowledge of a wide range of industries, and further adjustment made. All this means, therefore, that there are some estimated percentages marked *cir*, which are questionable and that some reader may know of one establishment in one southeastern state which will prove an estimate incorrect. It is believed, however, that in most cases the estimates are accurate enough to indicate whether the Southeast has had considerable, a fair amount, or very little experience in a given line of manufacturing. For the purpose of this study that is sufficient.

The other columns are, perhaps, clear enough from the use made of the indices in the preceding chapters. Some industries show a low index on one score and high on all others. Some which are very low by all measures are probably unsatisfactory for all concerned—labor, capital and the community. But even among these there are many individual companies which pay good wages and create good values. And certainly the industries which, by and large, offer employment opportunities to a wide range of skilled workers and technicians, pay good wages, spend much for raw materials and show high balance beyond bare operating expenses are community assets. Because they create more value there is more for everybody—the worker, the producer of raw materials, the tax gatherer and the investor.

The comparison of industries by any one or all indices furnishes food for thought about manufacturing in the United States along other lines besides those of regional development. The application of these indices reveals, for example, wide differences between monopolistic and highly competitive industries; between industries making products covered by patents and sold through elaborate advertising programs, and those making old line products manufactured without protection and sold without ballyhoo. The figures show great differences between new industries, on the one hand, which, because of invention and adaptation, are still in a stage requiring large numbers of engineers, technicians, and laboratory workers to plan, supervise, test and improve the process and the product, and old industries, on the other hand, where procedure is more or less stabilized and machinery, jobs, and product are standardized. They show vividly the differences between industries in which the processes are continuous with a few workers to handle large quantities of materials by turning valves, and those industries which require the human eye and hand at a hundred stages in production. They show equally vividly differences between the industries which require much skilled labor and those which require little. They show wide differences between industries in which labor is thoroughly organized and those which can draw from an inchoate mass of workers.

These statistics, moreover, suggest certain broad questions about our whole manufacturing economy. For example, some industries expend so large a proportion of their created values on the two items of salary and wages that there can be little left for other important purposes. And yet in many of these very industries the wages and salaries per wage earner are low. This state of affairs occurs most often in the industries making articles of common use and employing the greatest number of workers.

Because of this, workers get necessities cheaply because other workers and capital receive small return; but these same workers receive small wages because they must make cheaply those products on which they work—a vicious circle. For the full picture we need information on capital costs. But without exact figures on this item it is apparent that many of the industries making the great essential articles of clothing, shoes, materials for houses are almost, if not actually, marginal industries.

In contrast, other industries use small percentages of their created value for wages and salaries. Many of this type are found among the new industries. This poses an interesting question in economic theory: as industries grow older, expand, and become competitive with their products growing in general use, do they tend to work down toward minimum returns for labor and capital? Some of those using small percentage of the created value for wages and salaries make luxury products, especially cheap luxuries for the masses. This suggests an interesting question in social psychology: are people willing to pay proportionally more for, and to buy more consistently, their little luxuries than their chief necessities?

These tables—portraying the manufacturing of the United States in simplified fashion though they do—suggest many other questions. Why are salaries per salaried person apparently so much more uniform than wages per wage earner? Why is industry as a consumer apparently more willing to pay prices that mean a return to labor and capital than is the personal consumer? For example, bags other than paper is one of the highest index industries in the cutting-up group which includes all sorts of clothing; leather belting furnishes by far the highest indices in the leather group which includes boots and shoes for the nation. Why are there so many exceptions to a seemingly logical rule that industries with a high value added by manufacture will pay high wages or require large capital investment?

Most of these questions have a bearing on the place of the Southeast in the manufacturing economy of the nation. But their fuller analysis would belong to another and a larger study.

84 SOUTHERN INDUSTRY

INDICES OF MANUFACTURING INDUSTRIES, 1937—

	Industries	Total wage earners	Percent wage earners in S.E.	Wages per wage earner		Value of product per wage earner		Value added by manufacture per wage earner	
	FOOD AND KINDRED PRODUCTS								
1	Beverages nonalcoholic.....................	27,979	30.4	$ 1,107	963	$ 9,892	10,540	$ 5,876	6,149
2	Bread and other bakery products............	239,388	9.2	1,225	955	5,975	5,300	2,922	2,530
3	Butter....................................	19,437	4.8	1,009	820	30,342	24,277	4,100	4,206
4	Cheese...................................	4,482	5.8	973	821	25,164	18,103	3,818	3,382
5	Condensed and evaporated milk.............	8,967	10.0 cir	1,110		23,600		4,930	
6	Canned and dried fruits, vegetables, etc.......	137,064	11.3	676	357	5,756	2,901	2,118	1,054
7	Canned and cured fish, etc..................	18,229	26.0	478	284	4,301	2,160	1,628	905
8	Cereal preparations........................	8,133	2.0 cir	1,330		20,200		8,560	
9	Chewing gum.............................	2,401	2.0 cir	1,230		23,600		16,600	
10	Chocolate and cocoa products..............	7,402	0	1,100		13,600		3,810	
11	Confectionery.............................	53,722	8.4	809	621	5,693	5,238	2,291	2,081
12	Corn sirup, etc., and starch................	7,010	0	1,490		19,300		5,610	
13	Feeds, prepared, for animals................	14,397	12.5	1,100	708	28,840	19,982	5,328	3,904
14	Flavoring extracts and sirups...............	4,162	12.0 cir	1,030		28,300		17,200	
15	Flour and other grain mill products..........	26,390	14.5	1,144	763	32,448	20,278	5,063	3,358
16	Foods not elsewhere classified..............	16,794	8.6	915	582	16,592	11,584	4,634	3,084
17	Ice cream.................................	18,664	12.8	1,140	892	15,109	11,193	7,416	5,273
18	Manufactured ice..........................	18,705	26.4	1,155	870	7,300	6,306	5,829	4,965
19	Liquors distilled...........................	6,215	34.1	1,193	979	18,198	19,196	6,420	6,026
20	Liquors malt..............................	47,037	5.8	1,685	1,360	11,419	7,783	7,126	4,967
21	Liquors, rectified or blended................	7,094	4.1	949	795	20,363	18,648	10,160	9,736
22	Liquors vinous............................	3,005	2.0 cir	1,030		14,200		6,370	
23	Macaroni, etc.............................	6,452	5.0 cir	886		7,790		2,710	
24	Malt.....................................	1,644	0	1,770		57,189		11,250	
25	Meat Packing.............................	127,477	5.6	1,337	930	21,866	14,692	3,148	2,467
26	Oleomargarine not made in meat packing ests..	1,214	0	1,320		36,800		11,160	
27	Poultry dressing and packing................	8,913	4.0 cir	666		11,870		2,050	
28	Rice cleaning and polishing.................	2,218	67.0	611	474	21,124	17,579	3,623	2,565
29	Sausages, meat puddings, etc...............	9,342	8.0 cir	1,220		16,000		3,240	
30	Sausage casings...........................	875	0	1,030		7,460		2,430	
31	Shortening (except lard), cooking, salad oils....	4,901	15.0 cir	1,150		48,862		7,160	
32	Sugar, beet...............................	9,366	0	1,250		11,460		4,090	
33	Sugar, cane, production....................	4,221	100.0	565	565	6,920	6,920	1,995	1,995
34	Sugar, cane, refining.......................	14,024	27.0 cir	1,140		30,200		4,410	
35	Vinegar and cider..........................	974	No data	857		6,600		2,720	
	TOTAL........................	888,298	......	1,101		12,590		3,770	
	TEXTILES AND THEIR PRODUCTS								
	A. TEXTILE MILL PRODUCTS								
36	Carpets and rugs, paper, fiber, and grass......	788	0	975		4,000		2,451	
37	Carpets and rugs, rag......................	429	2.0 cir	654		3,115		1,607	
38	Carpets and rugs, wool....................	30,779	3.0 cir	1,045		5,207		2,554	
39	Carpet yarn...............................	2,584	0	1,151		6,521		1,975	
40	Cordage and twine........................	14,043	33.0 cir	832		4,730		2,022	
41	Jute goods................................	6,522	?	796		3,920		1,900	
42	Linen goods...............................	1,862	0	874		3,459		1,399	
43	Cotton goods woven (over 12 inches)........	336,104	74.0	761	729	2,877	2,881	1,313	1,277
44	Cotton narrow fabrics......................	12,616	7.0 cir	882		3,447		1,694	
45	Cotton yarn and thread....................	86,206	78.5	659	610	3,023	2,862	1,224	1,108
46	Fish nets and seines.......................	502	0	922		5,347		2,353	
47	Dyeing and finishing cotton fabrics...........	49,635	34.0 cir	987		4,111		1,972	
48	Dyeing and finishing rayon and silk...........	18,003	2.5 cir	1,091		3,199		1,932	
49	Dyeing and finishing yarn...................	7,344	35.0 cir	944		2,943		2,015	
50	Felt goods (except woven felts)..............	3,711	0	1,221		7,990		2,964	
51	Hat bodies—carded wool felt...............	4,038	2.5 cir	920		3,832		1,715	
52	Hats, fur-felt..............................	15,926	1.0 cir	1,112		4,193		2,012	
53	Hats, straw, men's........................	3,024	0	890		4,505		2,144	
54	Hats and caps, except felt and straw, men's....	3,460	1.0 cir	848		3,390		1,677	
55	Hat and cap materials, men's	2,444	0	881		6,226		2,097	
56	Hosiery...................................	150,460	44.2	906	714	2,403	2,137	1,340	1,109
57	Knitted underwear.........................	39,923	33.3	715	647	2,950	2,650	1,361	1,177
58	Knitted cloth..............................	11,360	7.0 cir	929		5,987		2,087	
59	Knitted outerwear, regular factories..........	23,424	2.5 cir	833		4,365		1,852	
60	Knitted outerwear, contract factories........	2,715	0	755		1,617		1,449	
61	Knitted gloves and mittens..................	3,182	0	667		1,821		1,089	
62	Lace goods................................	8,109	0	1,114		3,495		2,196	
63	Rayon woven goods (18 inches and over)......	57,949	36.0	845	794	3,965	3,806	1,391	1,279
64	Rayon narrow fabrics......................	5,568	8.0 cir	867		3,329		1,830	
65	Rayon throwing and spinning................	1,937	0	615		1,239		995	

Percentages of wage earners in the Southeast in italics and marked *cir* are estimated. For method see p. 81.

THE STATISTICAL PICTURE

United States and the Southeast

Percent wages are of value added by manufacture		Salary per salaried person		Salary per wage earner		Wage earners per salaried person		Wage and salary per wage earner		Percent wages and salary are of value added by manufacture		Balance per wage earner for interest, profits, taxes, etc.		
18.8	15.7	$ 2,301	2,646	$ 552	565	4.2	4.6	$ 1,659	1,528	28.3	25.0	$ 4,217	4,621	1
42.0	37.9	1,914	1,713	190	182	10.1	9.5	1,415	1,137	48.4	44.9	1,507	1,393	2
24.6	19.5	1,403	1,461	472	557	3.0	2.6	1,481	1,377	36.4	32.7	2,619	2,829	3
25.5	24.0	1,464	1,051	204	261	7.2	4.0	1,177	1,077	30.8	31.8	2,641	2,305	4
22.5		1,852		367		5.0		1,477		30.0		3,453		5
31.9	33.9	1,840	1,395	146	75	12.6	18.6	822	432	38.9	41.0	1,296	622	6
29.4	31.4	2,189	1,600	122	58	18.0	27.5	600	342	36.9	37.9	1,028	562	7
15.5		2,622		380		6.9		1,710		20.0		6,850		8
7.4		2,210		403		5.8		1,633		9.8		14,967		9
28.9		2,127		308		6.9		1,408		37.0		2,402		10
35.2	29.8	2,106	1,922	216	241	9.8	8.0	1,025	862	44.7	41.4	1,266	1,219	11
26.6		2,740		440		6.2		1,930		34.4		3,680		12
20.6	18.2	1,804	1,744	600	613	3.0	2.8	1,700	1,321	32.0	33.8	3,628	2,583	13
6.0		2,425		964		2.5		1,994		11.6		15,206		14
22.6	22.7	2,098	1,911	525	417	4.0	4.6	1,669	1,180	32.9	35.2	3,394	2,178	15
19.8	18.8	2,170	2,122	453	350	4.8	6.1	1,368	932	29.5	30.2	3,266	2,152	16
15.4	16.9	1,911	1,839	597	697	3.2	2.6	1,737	1,589	23.4	30.2	5,679	3,684	17
19.7	17.5	1,840	1,556	591	568	3.1	2.7	1,746	1,438	30.0	29.0	4,083	3,527	18
18.6	16.2	2,205	2,207	457	477	4.8	4.6	1,650	1,456	25.7	24.2	4,770	4,570	19
23.6	27.4	2,510	2,090	554	474	4.5	4.4	2,239	1,834	31.4	37.0	4,887	3,133	20
9.4	8.2	2,195	2,100	383	422	5.7	5.0	1,332	1,217	13.1	12.5	8,828	8,519	21
16.2		1,980		577		3.4		1,607		25.3		4,763		22
32.8		1,980		302		6.5		1,188		43.8		1,522		23
15.7		4,200		816		5.1		2,586		22.9		8,664		24
42.4	37.8	2,084	1,992	411	348	5.1	5.7	1,748	1,278	55.5	52.0	1,400	1,189	25
11.8		2,240		710		3.1		2,030		18.2		9,130		26
32.5		1,580		219		7.2		885		43.2		1,165		27
16.9	18.5	2,196	2,010	557	488	3.9	4.1	1,168	962	32.2	37.4	2,455	1,603	28
37.6		2,301		401		5.7		1,621		50.0		1,619		29
42.8		3,690		342		10.8		1,372		56.4		1,058		30
16.1		2,030		498		4.1		1,648		23.0		5,512		31
30.6		2,140		360		5.9		1,610		39.3		2,480		32
28.3	28.3	1,386	1,386	197	197	7.1	7.1	762	762	38.2	38.2	1,233	1,233	33
25.8		2,340		283		8.3		1,423		32.2		2,987		34
31.6		2,043		410		5.0		1,267		46.5		1,453		35
29.2		2,020		317		6.4		1,418		37.6		2,352		
39.8		2,341		309		7.6		1,284		52.4		1,167		36
40.7		1,550		163		9.5		817		50.9		790		37
41.0		2,184		163		13.4		1,208		47.3		1,346		38
58.3		3,398		189		17.9		1,340		67.8		635		39
41.2		2,479		211		11.8		1,043		51.6		979		40
41.8		2,551		181		14.1		977		51.4		923		41
62.5		2,193		202		10.8		1,076		76.8		323		42
58.0	57.0	2,406	2,437	60	52	40.3	46.6	821	781	62.5	61.2	492	496	43
52.1		2,646		234		11.3		1,116		65.8		578		44
53.8	55.1	2,164	2,155	79	55	27.4	39.1	738	665	60.2	60.1	486	443	45
39.2		1,952		408		4.8		1,330		56.6		1,023		46
50.0		2,374		253		9.4		1,240		62.8		732		47
56.4		2,558		281		9.1		1,372		71.0		560		48
46.9		2,844		316		9.0		1,260		62.5		755		49
41.2		2,330		272		8.6		1,493		50.4		1,471		50
53.6		1,889		108		17.4		1,028		60.0		687		51
55.3		2,412		154		15.6		1,266		63.0		746		52
41.5		2,198		249		8.8		1,139		53.1		1,005		53
50.6		1,783		223		8.0		1,071		63.8		606		54
42.0		2,918		270		10.8		1,151		55.0		946		55
67.6	64.5	2,236	2,321	100	78	22.2	29.5	1,006	792	75.2	71.5	334	317	56
52.5	55.0	2,157	2,262	144	94	15.0	24.1	859	741	63.0	63.0	502	436	57
44.6		2,355		260		9.0		1,189		56.9		898		58
45.0		2,313		260		8.9		1,093		59.0		759		59
52.1		2,217		93		23.8		848		58.6		601		60
61.3		2,456		93		26.3		760		69.8		329		61
50.7		2,262		245		9.2		1,359		62.0		837		62
60.8	62.1	2,160	1,994	91	57	23.7	35.0	936	851	67.2	66.6	455	428	63
47.4		2,273		201		11.3		1,068		58.3		762		64
61.8		2,036		101		20.2		716		72.0		279		65

Figures in bold-faced type are indices for the portion of the industry that is located in the Southeast.

SOUTHERN INDUSTRY

Indices of Manufacturing Industries, 1937—

	Industries	Total wage earners	Percent wage earners in S.E.	Wages per wage earner		Value of product per wage earner		Value added by manufacture per wage earner	
	A. TEXTILE MILL PRODUCTS (Cont.)								
66	Rayon yarn and thread (processed for sale)...	5,399	11.0 cir	$ 677		$ 4,025		$ 1,283	
67	Silk broad woven goods....................	17,597	12.0 cir	796		3,591		1,376	
68	Silk narrow fabrics.......................	4,527	1.0 cir	928		3,042		1,821	
69	Silk throwing and spinning (commission only)	13,290	4.0 cir	586		1,150		876	
70	Silk yarn and thread (made for sale)........	10,572	7.0 cir	740		3,798		1,205	
	TEXTILES AND THEIR PRODUCTS								
71	Processed waste..........................	5,560	8.0 cir	864		6,868		2,084	
72	Batting and padding......................	4,645	16.0 cir	937		7,938		2,795	
73	Woolen woven goods and woven felt.........	61,931	13.0 cir	1,011		4,662		1,868	
74	Woolen yarn.............................	2,749	3.0 cir	1,012		4,941		1,809	
75	Worsted woven goods.....................	70,227	2.0 cir	1,012		5,822		1,879	
76	Worsted yarn	17,303	1.0 cir	858		5,186		1,355	
77	Wool combing............................	3,252	0	1,032		3,167		1,761	
78	Wool scouring............................	1,252	0	1,113		3,635		2,104	
79	Woolen and worsted dyeing and finishing.....	2,563	0	1,095		4,316		2,492	
	TOTAL.......................	1,125,514	....	851		3,543		1,540	
	B. THE CUTTING-UP INDUSTRIES								
80	Men's & boys' clothing, not elsw. clsfd., reg.*	94,361	10.0 cir	1,071		5,924		2,174	
81	Men's & boys' clothing, not elsw. clsfd., cont.†	43,953	.2 cir	938		1,347		1,244	
82	Men's & boys' clothing, leather and sheep lined	4,075	0	913		5,147		1,613	
83	Men's & boys' work & sport cloth., not leather.	69,502	35.3	594	481	2,941	2,604	1,029	788
84	Men's & boys' trousers, wash suits, etc. apparel	15,817	25.0 cir	603		2,957		1,081	
85	Shirts (except work), collars, nightwear, reg...	55,570	13.0 cir	629		3,149		1,298	
86	Shirts (except work), collars, nightwear, cont..	12,024	1.0 cir	508		768		667	
87	Men's & boys' underwear, reg...............	7,888	18.0 cir	534		2,572		834	
88	Men's & boys' underwear, cont..............	1,424	0	437		639		535	
89	Men's furnishing goods, not elsw. clsfd., reg...	12,144	2.0 cir	806		4,946		1,893	
90	Men's furnishing goods, not elsw. clsfd., cont..	759	0	703		1,125		1,018	
91	Handkerchiefs, reg........................	4,065	10.0 cir	627		4,619		1,305	
92	Handkerchiefs, cont.......................	932	0	629		1,013		869	
93	Suspenders, garters, etc....................	2,903	1.0 cir	755		5,180		2,197	
94	Gloves and mittens, cloth or cloth and leather.	12,679	9.0 cir	619		2,568		1,093	
95	Blouses, reg..............................	3,850	0	870		6,957		2,600	
96	Blouses, cont.............................	2,554	0	650		955		896	
97	Clothing, women's & misses, not elsw. c., reg..	26,897	1.0 cir	766		5,575		2,141	
98	Clothing, women's & misses, not elsw. c., cont..	5,178	0	638		1,006		918	
99	Coats, suits, etc., women's & misses, reg......	20,690	.5 cir	1,436		14,022		4,281	
100	Coats, suits, etc., women's & misses, cont.....	18,923	0	1,163		1,643		1,529	
101	Dresses, except house, reg..................	48,217	.5 cir	1,126		8,360		2,170	
102	Dresses, except house, cont.................	43,874	1.0 cir	972		1,333		1,273	
103	Dresses, house, uniforms, etc., reg...........	28,250	1.0 cir	608		3,324		1,353	
104	Dresses, house, uniforms, etc., cont..........	4,039	1.0 cir	545		803		734	
105	Outerwear, children's, reg..................	15,962	3.0 cir	833		4,857		1,929	
106	Outerwear, children's, cont.................	5,157	3.0 cir	641		958		905	
107	Underwear, women's and children's knitted...	10,453	4.0 cir	628		3,480		1,431	
108	Underwear, women's and children's woven.....	8,835	2.0 cir	624		3,401		1,183	
109	Millinery, reg.............................	21,321	4.0 cir	1,063		4,106		2,190	
110	Millinery, cont............................	239	0	1,120		2,917		2,280	
111	Corsets and allied garments.................	16,385	1.0 cir	809		4,320		2,336	
112	Awnings, tents, sails, canvas covers..........	4,732	8.0	1,024	961	6,408	5,565	2,709	2,626
113	Bags, other than paper.....................	12,075	30.0 cir	807		10,766		2,176	
114	Curtains, draperies, and bedspreads, reg......	8,934	20.0 cir	661		5,878		1,709	
115	Curtains, draperies, and bedspreads, cont.....	711	0	712		1,560		1,317	
116	Flags, banners, vestments, and robes.........	2,146	1.0 cir	756		3,667		1,926	
117	House furnishings not elsewhere classified....	11,346	8.0 cir	813		6,116		2,175	
118	Fabricated textile products not elsw. clsfd.....	2,903	3.0 cir	990		6,810		2,826	
	TOTAL.......................	661,767	....	851		4,390		1,751	
	C. THE PROCESSING INDUSTRIES								
119	Embroideries – Schiffli machine, reg.........	1,171	0	853		4,457		2,081	
120	Embroideries – Schiffli machine, cont........	1,586	0	894		3,133		2,081	
121	Embroideries – other than Schiffli, reg.......	548	0	838		2,978		1,744	
122	Embroideries – other than Schiffli, cont......	3,394	.5 cir	842		2,050		1,616	
123	Trimmings (not made in textile mills), reg....	4,362	1.0 cir	850		6,943		2,303	
124	Trimmings (not made in textile mills), cont. ..	4,128	0	938		2,143		1,805	
125	Artificial leather..........................	2,541	0	1,368		10,865		3,618	
126	Oilcloth.................................	1,269	0	1,338		10,100		2,713	
127	Asphalted-felt-base floor covering............	3,280	0	1,455		10,228		..4,853	
128	Linoleum................................	4,827	0	1,368		7,383		4,218	
	TOTAL.......................	27,106	....	1,105		6,180		2,902	

*Reg. denotes regular factories.   †Cont. denotes contract factories.
Percentages of wage earners in the Southeast in italics and marked *cir* are estimated. For method see p. 81.

THE STATISTICAL PICTURE

UNITED STATES AND THE SOUTHEAST *(Continued)*

Percent wages are of value added by manufacture	Salary per salaried person		Salary per wage earner		Wage earners per salaried person		Wage and salary per wage earner		Percent wages and salary are of value added by manufacture		Balance per wage earner for interest, profits, taxes, etc.		
52.8	$ 2,402		$ 157		15.2		$ 834		65.0		$ 449		66
57.9	1,919		117		16.4		913		66.4		463		67
51.0	2,684		232		11.6		1,160		63.6		661		68
67.0	2,005		87		23.1		673		76.9		203		69
61.5	2,360		115		20.5		855		71.0		350		70
41.5	2,657		313		8.5		1,177		56.4		907		71
33.5	2,852		358		8.0		1,295		46.3		1,500		72
54.2	2,886		170		17.0		1,181		63.2		687		73
55.9	3,006		248		12.1		1,260		69.7		549		74
53.9	2,459		141		17.5		1,153		61.4		726		75
63.3	2,971		127		23.3		985		72.6		370		76
58.6	4,755		143		33.2		1,175		66.6		586		77
52.8	2,800		412		6.8		1,525		72.4		579		78
44.0	3,222		481		6.7		1,576		63.2		916		79
55.2	2,392		125		19.1		976		63.2		564		
49.4	2,257		221		10.2		1,292		59.5		882		80
75.4	2,262		69		32.6		1,007		80.6		237		81
56.6	2,038		220		9.3		1,133		70.2		480		82
57.8	**61.1**	1,808	1,687	94	60	19.2	28.3	688	541	67.0	68.6	341	247	83
55.7	2,022		134		15.1		737		68.1		344		84
48.4	1,800		103		17.4		732		56.4		566		85
76.4	1,857		46		40.1		554		83.0		113		86
64.0	1,973		93		21.2		627		75.2		207		87
81.6	1,383		33		41.9		470		87.8		65		88
42.6	2,149		216		10.0		1,022		54.0		871		89
69.2	1,526		32		47.4		735		72.2		283		90
48.0	2,071		147		14.1		774		59.3		531		91
72.5	2,479		61		40.5		690		79.4		179		92
34.4	2,131		252		8.5		1,007		45.8		1,190		93
56.6	1,703		57		29.8		676		61.9		417		94
33.5	1,930		255		7.6		1,125		43.2		1,475		95
72.5	2,179		60		36.0		710		79.2		186		96
35.7	2,124		222		9.6		988		46.0		1,153		97
69.5	1,743		46		38.1		684		74.5		234		98
33.5	2,401		509		4.7		1,945		45.4		2,336		99
76.2	2,032		76		26.6		1,239		81.0		290		100
51.9	2,542		369		6.9		1,495		68.9		675		101
76.3	2,352		64		36.7		1,036		81.2		237		102
45.0	1,928		129		15.0		737		54.5		616		103
74.4	1,422		40		35.7		585		79.6		149		104
43.2	2,145		211		10.2		1,044		54.1		885		105
70.8	1,801		49		36.6		690		76.2		215		106
43.9	2,089		134		15.5		762		53.2		669		107
52.6	1,950		118		16.4		742		62.7		441		108
48.6	2,286		285		8.0		1,348		61.4		842		109
49.1	2,152		333		6.4		1,453		63.5		827		110
34.7	2,154		296		7.3		1,105		47.3		1,231		111
37.8	**36.6**	2,081	2,034	586	640	3.5	3.2	1,610	1,601	59.5	60.8	1,099	1,025	112
37.2	2,483		282		8.8		1,089		50.0		1,087		113
38.7	2,053		253		8.1		914		53.5		795		114
54.1	1,498		112		7.3		824		62.6		493		115
39.3	2,000		340		5.9		1,096		56.8		830		116
37.4	2,038		295		6.9		1,108		51.0		1,067		117
35.1	2,371		305		7.7		1,295		45.8		1,531		118
48.6	2,180		181		12.1		1,032		58.9		719		
40.9	2,464		276		8.9		1,129		54.1		952		119
43.0	2,973		283		10.5		1,177		56.5		904		120
48.2	2,354		284		8.3		1,122		64.2		622		121
52.1	1,942		164		11.9		1,006		62.2		610		122
36.9	2,212		406		5.4		1,256		54.5		1,047		123
52.0	2,290		235		9.8		1,173		65.0		632		124
37.8	2,840		452		6.3		1,820		50.4		1,798		125
49.4	1,573		286		5.5		1,624		59.8		1,089		126
30.0	2,658		230		11.5		1,685		34.7		3,168		127
32.4	2,077		190		10.9		1,558		37.0		2,660		128
38.1	2,310		273		8.4		1,378		47.5		1,524		

Figures in bold-faced type are indices of the portion of the industry that is located in the Southeast.

SOUTHERN INDUSTRY

Indices of Manufacturing Industries, 1937—

	Industries	Total wage earners	Percent wage earners in S.E.	Wages per wage earner		Value of product per wage earner		Value added by manufacture per wage earner	
	Forest Products								
129	Baskets and willow ware................	9,308	39.0 cir	$ 551		$ 1,789		$ 1,041	
130	Billiard and pool tables, bowling alleys, etc....	530	2.0 cir	1,015		10,467		6,998	
131	Boxes, cigar........................	3,296	26.0 cir	704		2,163		1,349	
132	Boxes, wooden, except cigar............	25,981	39.6	752	498	3,323	2,124	1,574	1,058
133	Caskets, coffins, etc...................	13,678	13.7	1,105	797	5,246	3,921	2,788	1,727
134	Cooperage..........................	9,588	35.0 cir	957		5,238		1,846	
135	Cork products.......................	3,599	3.0 cir	1,151		6,061		2,192	
136	Excelsior............................	960	23.0 cir	760		3,160		1,769	
137	Furniture (household)*...............	130,765	22.7	947	758	3,614	3,080	1,855	1,505
138	Furniture, other, office, etc............	39,307	....	1,241		4,728		2,736	
139	Lasts and related products.............	1,444	0	1,269		3,763		2,638	
140	Lumber and timber products...........	323,928	44.5	849	532	2,619	1,955	1,555	1,120
141	Matches............................	5,261	4.0 cir	1,025		5,874		2,032	
142	Mirror and picture frames.............	3,382	1.0 cir	1,015		3,775		2,228	
143	Planing mill products.................	66,814	28.2	1,014	702	4,678	3,850	2,062	1,516
144	Synthetic-resin, etc., products.........	16,673	.4 cir	1,189		4,661		2,739	
145	Turpentine and rosin.................	1,506	100.0	232	232	19,273	19,273	4,220	4,220
146	Window and door screens and weather strip...	2,833	15.0 cir	1,071		5,206		2,596	
147	Wood preserving.....................	12,401	34.0 cir	914		9,410		2,582	
148	Wood turned and shaped..............	23,087	27.4	844	707	3,044	2,688	1,621	1,300
	Total.......................	694,341	....	918		3,510		1,825	
	Paper and Allied Products								
149	Pulp (wood and other fiber)..........	26,994	25.0 cir	1,244		9,157		3,465	
150	Paper..............................	110,809	7.0 cir	1,282		8,645		3,524	
151	Bags (paper) not made in paper mills....	10,360	26.0 cir	951		7,959		2,803	
152	Boxes, paper........................	65,158	5.0 cir	1,013		7,205		2,624	
153	Cardboard, not made in paper mills.....	877	0	928		6,133		2,798	
154	Card cutting and designing............	3,315	0	1,248		6,376		3,550	
155	Envelopes..........................	9,511	4.0 cir	1,104		5,393		2,753	
156	Paper goods not elsewhere classified.....	32,888	5.0 cir	1,059		7,881		3,448	
157	Wall paper.........................	4,543	0	1,201		5,893		3,269	
	Total.......................	264,455	....	1,161		7,800		3,230	
	Printing, Publishing and Allied Industries								
158	Newspaper and periodical.............	135,215	8.9	1,641	1,351	10,325	7,450	7,418	5,707
159	Book, music, and job printing..........	141,368	6.2	1,380	1,152	5,728	4,550	3,722	2,855
160	Bookbinding and blank-book making....	25,333	4.0 cir	1,132		3,743		2,529	
161	Engraving, chasing, etching, etc.........	2,152	0	1,288		4,127		2,795	
162	Engraving, steel, copper, wood.........	7,831	3.0 cir	1,262		3,759		3,489	
163	Lithographing.......................	24,079	2.0 cir	1,492		5,721		3,464	
164	Photoengraving, not in printing establishments.	12,364	4.5	2,355	1,928	6,305	5,548	5,068	4,397
165	Stereotyping & Electrotyping, not in prtg. est..	4,766	1.0 cir	2,034		6,513		5,432	
	Total.......................	353,108	....	1,510		7,325		5,100	
	Chemicals and Allied Products								
166	Ammunition and related products.......	6,596	0	1,150		5,677		3,181	
167	Baking powder, yeast, etc.............	2,380	3.0 cir	1,580		12,722		7,122	
168	Blacking, stains, and dressings..........	1,536	6.0 cir	963		12,489		7,288	
169	Bluing..............................	67	2.0 cir	1,032		16,844		11,614	
170	Bone black, carbon black, etc..........	2,190	19.3	1,238	1,058	8,609	6,299	5,305	3,532
171	Candles............................	725	0	946		7,381		3,762	
172	Chemicals not elsewhere classified.......	78,951	9.7	1,485	1,176	11,814	11,900	6,050	6,463
173	Cleaning and polishing preparations.....	3,341	1.0 cir	1,180		17,322		10,245	
174	Compressed and liquefied gases	4,655	7.0 cir	1,416		12,120		9,060	
175	Drug grinding.......................	699	.8 cir	1,215		11,352		4,539	
176	Drugs and medicines.................	24,095	5.5	1,084	732	14,356	12,482	10,255	8,303
177	Explosives..........................	5,406	1.0 cir	1,595		10,762		6,284	
178	Fertilizers..........................	20,893	62.3	735	539	9,370	8,608	3,144	2,660
179	Fireworks...........................	1,760	0	921		4,618		2,519	
180	Glue and gelatin.....................	3,547	1.0 cir	1,287		11,460		4,866	
181	Grease and tallow...................	5,200	2.0 cir	1,301		10,052		3,709	
182	Ink, printing........................	2,793	1.5 cir	1,463		16,952		7,964	
183	Ink, writing.........................	366	0	1,012		9,496		5,398	
184	Insecticides, etc......................	4,322	10.0 cir	1,078		16,467		8,576	
185	Mucilage, etc........................	295	0	1,062		14,270		6,931	

*Household and other than household are combined for regional figures. Since Southeast makes mostly household furniture comparison is made with that part of the industry.
Percentages of wage earners in the Southeast in italics and marked *cir* are estimated. For method see p. 81.

THE STATISTICAL PICTURE

UNITED STATES AND THE SOUTHEAST *(Continued)*

Percent wages are of value added by manufacture		Salary per salaried person		Salary per wage earner		Wage earners per salaried person		Wage and salary per wage earner		Percent wages and salary are of value added by manufacture		Balance per wage earner for interest, profits, taxes, etc.		
52.9		$ 2,079		$ 127		16.3		$ 678		65.1		$ 363		129
14.5		2,206		246		9.0		1,261		18.0		5,737		130
52.2		2,624		152		17.2		856		63.5		493		131
47.8	47.1	2,244	2,304	172	105	13.1	22.0	924	603	58.7	57.0	650	455	132
39.7	46.0	2,414	2,321	426	330	5.7	7.05	1,531	1,127	54.9	65.2	1,257	600	133
51.9		2,435		167		14.6		1,124		60.9		722		134
52.5		2,348		271		8.6		1,422		64.9		770		135
43.0		2,102		169		12.5		929		52.5		840		136
51.1	50.3	2,133	2.249	210	157	10.1	14.3	1,157	915	62.4	60.8	698	590	137
45.5		2,183		352		6.2		1,593		58.2		1,143		138
48.2		2,560		463		5.5		1,732		65.7		906		139
54.6	47.5	2,166	2,043	107	92	20.2	22.1	956	624	61.5	55.7	599	496	140
50.4		2,029		167		12.2		1,192		58.7		840		141
45.6		2,271		361		6.3		1,376		61.8		852		142
49.1	46.4	1,988	1,818	296	201	6.7	9.05	1,310	903	63.5	59.6	752	613	143
43.4		2,313		292		7.9		1,481		54.1		1,258		144
5.5	5.5	664	664	577	577	1.2	1.2	809	809	19.2	19.2	3,411	3,411	145
41.3		2,239		387		5.8		1,458		56.2		1,136		146
35.4		2,056		157		13.1		1,071		41.5		1,511		147
52.0	54.4	2,107	2,085	206	153	10.2	13.5	1,050	860	64.8	66.2	571	440	148
50.4		2,120		183		11.6		1,101		60.4		724		
35.9		2,392		191		12.5		1,435		41.4		2,030		149
36.3		2,714		287		9.4		1,569		44.5		1,955		150
33.9		2,693		265		10.2		1,216		43.4		1,587		151
38.5		2,512		344		7.3		1,357		51.7		1,267		152
33.2		2,837		721		3.9		1,649		58.9		1,149		153
35.1		2,210		375		5.9		1,623		45.7		1,927		154
40.1		2,522		448		5.6		1,552		56.4		1,201		155
30.7		2,351		421		5.6		1,480		42.9		1,968		156
36.7		2,641		365		7.2		1,566		47.9		1,703		157
36.0		2,552		317		8.1		1,478		45.7		1,752		
22.1	23.7	1,918	1,570	2,024	1,658	0.9	0.95	3,665	3,009	49.4	52.7	3,753	2,698	158
37.2	40.4	2,293	1,980	702	533	3.3	3.7	2,082	1,685	55.9	59.2	1,640	1,170	159
44.7		2,393		409		5.8		1,541		60.9		988		160
46.0		2,293		460		5.0		1,748		62.5		1,047		161
36.2		2,476		544		4.5		1,806		51.8		1,683		162
43.1		2,754		663		4.2		2,155		62.2		1,309		163
46.4	43.9	2,778	2,642	1,020	978	2.7	2.7	3,375	2,906	66.6	66.2	1,693	1,491	164
37.5		2,943		1,078		2.7		3,112		57.3		2,320		165
29.6		2,062		1,198		1.7		2,708		53.1		2,392		
36.2		, 2,174		, 239		9.1		, 1,389		43.7		, 1,792		166
22.2		2,609		593		4.4		2,173		30.5		4,949		167
13.2		2,420		1,075		2.2		2,038		28.0		5,250		168
8.9		3,316		1,237		2.7		2,269		19.5		9,345		169
23.3	30.0	2,682	3,175	252	135	10.6	23.4	1,490	1,193	28.1	33.8	3,815	2,339	170
25.1		2,520		618		4.1		1,564		41.5		2,198		171
24.5	18.2	2,584	2,295	552	371	4.7	6.2	2,037	1,547	33.7	23.9	4,013	4,916	172
11.5		2,432		1,090		2.2		2,270		22.2		7,975		173
15.6		2,056		674		3.0		2,090		23.1		6,970		174
26.8		3,851		589		6.5		1,804		39.7		2,735		175
10.5	8.8	2,324	2,002	949	1,055	2.4	1.9	2,033	1,787	19.8	21.5	8,222	6,516	176
25.4		2,662		381		7.0		1,976		31.4		4,308		177
23.4	20.3	1,902	1,742	305	271	6.2	6.5	1,040	810	33.1	30.5	2,104	1,850	178
36.6		2,620		301		8.7		1,222		48.5		1,297		179
26.4		2,986		515		5.8		1,802		37.0		3,064		180
35.0		2,573		434		5.9		1,735		46.8		1,974		181
18.4		2,807		1,140		2.5		2,603		32.7		5,361		182
18.7		2,221		601		3.7		1,613		29.9		3,785		183
12.5		2,314		1,314		1.8		2,392		27.9		6,184		184
15.3		2,293		1,430		1.6		2,492		36.0		4,439		185

Figures in bold-faced type are indices for the portion of the industry that is located in the Southeast.

SOUTHERN INDUSTRY

INDICES OF MANUFACTURING INDUSTRIES, 1937—

	Industries	Total wage earners	Percent wage earners in S.E.	Wages per wage earner		Value of product per wage earner		Value added by manufacture per wage earner	
	CHEMICALS AND ALLIED PRODUCTS (Cont.)								
186	Oil, cottonseed, etc.	16,583	68.0	$ 514	495	$14,596	14,765	$ 2,792	2,522
187	Oils, essential	195	7.0 cir	1,362		20,416		5,373	
188	Oils not elsewhere classified	2,474	10.0 cir	1,197		28,083		5,402	
189	Paints, pigments and varnish	31,664	4.7	1,350	1,050	17,005	14,455	7,149	6,198
190	Perfumes, cosmetics, etc.	10,158	3.0 cir	912		13,028		7,721	
191	Rayon and allied products	55,098	45.0 cir	1,185		4,623		3,159	
192	Salt	4,616	15.0 cir	1,144		7,093		4,664	
193	Soap	14,008	2.0 cir	1,362		21,509		8,290	
194	Tanning materials, etc.	2,812	40.0 cir	1,067		12,690		4,652	
195	Wood distillation	4,467	68.0 cir	901		5,853		3,317	
196	Linseed oil and cake	2,628	0	1,367		34,382		6,041	
	TOTAL	314,520	....	1,212		11,830		5,700	
	PRODUCTS OF PETROLEUM AND COAL								
197	Coke oven products	20,603	11.0 cir	1,607		17,350		4,097	
198	Fuel briquets	457	5.0 cir	1,197		13,430		4,588	
199	Lubricating oils (not made in petrol. refineries)	2,231	2.0 cir	1,273		19,773		8,393	
200	Petroleum refining	83,182	6.0 cir	1,688		30,616		5,800	
	TOTAL	106,473	....	1,665		27,750		5,510	
	RUBBER PRODUCTS								
201	Rubber tires and tubes	63,290	1.0 cir	1,528		9,099		3,302	
202	Rubber boots and shoes	18,356	0	1,113		3,511		2,015	
203	Rubber goods (other than above)	48,172	?	1,125		5,039		2,549	
	TOTAL	129,818	....	1,321		6,810		2,843	
	LEATHER AND ITS MANUFACTURES								
204	Leather, tanned, etc., regular factories	48,132	5.0 cir	1,212		8,059		2,258	
205	Leather, tanned, etc., contract factories	2,555	0	1,157		2,784		1,890	
206	Leather, belting and packing	2,829	8.0 cir	1,186		9,862		4,373	
207	Boot and shoe cut stock	18,755	.3 cir	951		7,073		1,955	
208	Boots and shoes, other than rubber	215,438	5.0 cir	888		3,566		1,634	
209	Gloves and mittens, leather	11,637	0	777		2,640		1,289	
210	Handbags and purses, women's	11,306	1.0 cir	801		3,843		1,653	
211	Leather goods, small articles	2,443	0	757		4,182		1,996	
212	Leather goods, not elsewhere classified	7,103	1.0 cir	901		4,376		2,169	
213	Saddlery, harness, and whips	3,049	4.0 cir	885		4,400		1,740	
214	Trunks, suitcases, and bags	8,708	?	971		4,446		2,088	
	TOTAL	331,955	....	938		4,505		1,786	
	STONE, CLAY AND GLASS PRODUCTS								
215	Abrasives	9,670	1.0 cir	1,474		8,060		5,027	
216	Asbestos products other than steam pack., etc.	13,023	8.0 cir	1,087		4,899		2,634	
217	Cement	26,426	4.0 cir	1,289		6,933		4,284	
218	China firing not done in potteries	306	0	1,174		5,523		3,024	
219	Clay products other than pottery	59,585	18.9	971	686	2,740	2,162	1,884	1,407
220	Pottery and porcelain	33,060	3.0 cir	1,159		2,865		2,071	
221	Concrete products	12,840	13.5	1,073	787	5,933	4,250	3,171	2,220
222	Glass	79,585	4.0 cir	1,285		4,905		3,125	
223	Graphite, ground and refined	56	0	1,320		19,242		6,231	
224	Gypsum products	5,207	2.0 cir	1,266		8,184		4,981	
225	Wallboard, plaster, insulation, etc.	6,383	10.0 cir	1,048		6,431		3,979	
226	Lime	9,751	24.0 cir	986		3,592		2,229	
227	Marble, granite, etc., cut and shaped	20,816	22.5	1,171	876	3,795	2,753	2,482	1,930
228	Minerals and earths, ground, etc.	4,539	25.0 cir	1,079		4,662		3,425	
229	Mirrors, etc.	12,652	5.0 cir	1,105		6,956		3,736	
230	Nonclay refractories	5,641	2.0 cir	1,122		5,045		2,822	
231	Sand-lime brick	414	2.0 cir	1,112		3,908		2,591	
232	Statuary and art goods (factory)	858	1.0 cir	1,312		3,883		2,699	
	TOTAL	300,278	....	1,163		4,650		2,910	
	IRON AND STEEL AND THEIR PRODUCTS— NOT INCLUDING MACHINERY								
233	Blast-furnace products	23,075	10.0 cir	1,647		29,145		5,532	
234	Boiler shop products	24,485	10.0 cir	1,382		6,750		3,361	
235	Bolts, nuts, etc., not made in rolling mills	16,840	1.0 cir	1,312		5,824		3,191	
236	Cast iron pipe and fittings	17,613	60.0 cir	1,027		3,470		2,026	
237	Cutlery (not silver & plated) and edge tools	16,830	2.0 cir	1,107		4,052		2,939	

Percentages of wage earners in the Southeast in italics and marked *cir* are estimated. For method see p. 81.

THE STATISTICAL PICTURE

UNITED STATES AND THE SOUTHEAST (Continued)

Percent wages are of value added by manufacture		Salary per salaried person		Salary per wage earner		Wage earners per salaried person		Wage and salary per wage earner		Percent wages and salary are of value added by manufacture		Balance per wage earner for interest, profits, taxes, etc.		
18.4	19.6	$ 2,028	2,063	$ 341	305	6.0	6.8	$ 855	800	30.6	31.7	$ 1,937	1,722	186
25.3		3,110		1,020		3.0		2,382		44.3		2,991		187
22.1		2,652		580		4.6		1,777		32.9		3,625		188
18.9	17.0	2,378	2,670	901	1,090	2.6	2.4	2,251	2,140	31.5	34.6	4,898	4,058	189
11.8		2,152		616		3.5		1,528		19.8		6,193		190
37.5		2,239		210		10.6		1,395		44.2		1,764		191
24.6		2,615		276		9.2		1,420		30.4		3,244		192
16.4		2,128		550		3.9		1,912		23.1		6,378		193
22.9		2,893		859		3.4		1,926		41.4		2,726		194
27.1		1,914		239		8.0		1,140		34.4		2,177		195
22.6		2,316		204		11.4		1,571		26.0		4,470		196
21.3		2,372		535		4.4		1,747		30.6		3,953		
39.2		2,698		276		9.8		1,883		46.0		2,214		197
26.1		1,873		283		6.6		1,480		32.2		3,108		198
15.2		2,400		1,107		2.2		2,380		28.4		6,013		199
29.1		2,384		438		5.4		2,126		36.6		3,674		200
30.0		2,418		420		5.8		2,085		38.3		3,425		
46.2		2,312		400		5.8		1,928		58.4		1,374		201
55.3		1,778		230		7.7		1,343		66.6		672		202
44.1		2,269		321		7.1		1,446		56.7		1,103		203
46.4		2,235		347		6.4		1,668		58.6		1,175		
53.7		2,845		206		13.8		1,418		62.8		840		204
61.2		3,218		325		9.9		1,482		78.4		408		205
27.1		2,422		535		4.5		1,721		39.4		2,652		206
48.6		2,184		236		9.3		1,187		60.7		768		207
54.4		1,950		135		14.5		1,023		62.6		611		208
60.4		1,778		142		12.5		919		71.3		370		209
48.5		2,376		195		12.2		996		60.2		657		210
37.9		2,034		219		9.3		976		48.9		1,020		211
41.5		2,076		298		7.0		1,199		55.3		970		212
50.8		1,772		239		7.4		1,124		64.6		616		213
46.4		2,166		249		8.7		1,220		58.4		868		214
52.6		2,147		166		12.8		1,104		61.8		682		
29.3		2,651		468		5.7		1,942		38.6		3,085		215
41.3		2,083		227		9.2		1,314		49.9		1,320		216
30.1		2,467		252		9.8		1,541		36.0		2,743		217
38.8		2,736		381		7.0		1,555		51.4		1,469		218
51.5	48.8	2,102	2,272	172	150	12.2	15.2	1,143	836	60.7	59.4	741	571	219
56.0		2,467		196		12.6		1,355		65.4		716		220
33.9	35.4	2,046	1,966	390	342	5.2	5.8	1,463	1,129	46.1	50.8	1,708	1,091	221
41.1		2,238		225		9.9		1,510		48.3		1,615		222
21.2		3,283		1,407		2.3		2,727		43.8		3,504		223
25.4		2,186		274		8.0		1,540		30.9		3,441		224
26.5		1,824		274		6.7		1,322		33.2		2,657		225
44.2		2,017		160		12.6		1,146		51.4		1,083		226
47.1	45.4	1,924	1,758	327	232	5.9	7.6	1,498	1,108	60.4	57.4	984	822	227
31.5		2,477		378		6.6		1,457		42.5		1,968		228
29.6		2,181		309		7.1		1,414		37.8		2,322		229
39.7		2,542		157		16.2		1,279		45.3		1,543		230
43.0		1,981		330		6.0		1,442		55.6		1,149		231
48.6		2,157		425		5.1		1,737		64.4		962		232
40.0		2,209		241		9.2		1,404		48.2		1,506		
29.8		2,945		237		12.4		1,884		34.0		3,648		233
41.2		2,224		493		4.5		1,875		55.8		1,486		234
41.1		2,641		359		7.4		1,671		52.4		1,520		235
50.6		2,379		164		14.5		1,191		58.8		835		236
37.7		2,400		274		8.8		1,381		47.0		1,558		237

Figures in bold-faced type are indices for the portion of the industry that is located in the Southeast.

SOUTHERN INDUSTRY

INDICES OF MANUFACTURING INDUSTRIES, 1937—

	Industries	Total wage earners	Percent wage earners in S.E.	Wages per wage earner		Value of product per wage earner		Value added by manufacture per wage earner	
	IRON AND STEEL AND THEIR PRODUCTS (Cont.)								
238	Doors, shutters, sash frames, etc.............	8,408	3.0 cir	$ 1,413		$ 5,937		$ 3,552	
239	Files..	3,715	0	1,296		3,675		2,775	
240	Firearms.....................................	6,847	0	1,412		3,148		2,515	
241	Forgings, not made in rolling mills..........	18,255	1.0 cir	1,515		6,729		3,265	
242	Foundry products.............................	120,024	4.0	1,321	964	3,310	3,082	2,129	1,877
243	Galvanizing and other coating................	1,119	1.0 cir	1,230		5,357		3,098	
244	Hardware not elsewhere classified............	53,000	1.0 cir	1,232		4,134		2,497	
245	Heating and cook. app. except electric.......	89,287	9.7	1,252	865	4,920	2,724	2,903	1,558
246	Nails, spikes, etc., not made in rolling mills...	2,432	0	1,129		4,905		2,588	
247	Plumbers' supplies (not pipe or vitreous china).	25,240	4.0 cir	1,214		4,513		2,528	
248	Safes and vaults..............................	1,132	0	1,277		4,549		2,784	
249	Saws...	4,384	2.0 cir	1,272		4,528		2,837	
250	Screw-machine products and wood screws....	21,287	0	1,317		4,826		2,819	
251	Springs, steel, except wire, not in rolling mills.	3,902	0	1,487		6,979		2,840	
252	Stamped and pressed metal products..........	61,092	2.0 cir	1,197		4,813		2,388	
253	Steel barrels, kegs, and drums................	6,231	5.0 cir	1,181		7,732		2,869	
254	Steel-works and rolling mill products.........	479,342	4.0 cir	1,627		6,948		3,123	
255	Structural & ornamental steel, not in roll. mills	38,814	9.6	1,389	1,105	7,542	6,327	3,171	2,652
256	Tin cans and other tinware....................	33,145	4.0 cir	1,122		10,825		3,430	
257	Miscellaneous hand tools......................	17,612	.5 cir	1,200		4,545		2,787	
258	Wire drawn from purchased rods...............	24,580	0	1,382		7,329		3,327	
259	Wirework not elsewhere classified.............	33,471	1.0 cir	1,171		4,915		2,576	
260	Wrought pipe, not made in rolling mills.......	14,125	0	1,376		8,054		3,196	
	TOTAL......................................	1,166,287	....	1,428		6,420		2,940	
	NONFERROUS METALS AND THEIR PRODUCTS								
261	Aluminum products............................	23,695	1.0 cir	1,346		6,991		2,935	
262	Clocks, watches, time recording devices......	23,223	0	1,187		4,217		2,562	
263	Collapsible tubes.............................	1,983	0	944		4,632		1,973	
264	Electroplating................................	8,256	1.0 cir	1,190		3,232		2,407	
265	Fire extinguishers, chemical..................	1,041	0	1,346		8,539		5,098	
266	Gold leaf and foil.............................	625	0	824		3,679		1,709	
267	Gold, silver, & platinum-refining & alloying...	1,085	0	1,438		84,879		6,346	
268	Jewelry.......................................	20,368	.3 cir	1,143		4,743		2,587	
269	Jewelers' findings and materials..............	2,470	0	1,230		8,760		2,880	
270	Lighting equipment...........................	21,743	.1 cir	1,146		5,294		2,737	
271	Needles, pins, hooks and eyes, fasteners......	9,580	0	1,060		3,783		2,709	
272	Nonferrous alloys & prod., except aluminum..	83,016	.4 cir	1,391		8,063		3,333	
273	Smelting & refining nonferrous metals........	4,973	1.0 cir	1,201		22,724		3,812	
274	Sheet-metal work not specifically classified....	22,973	5.6	1,274	948	6,925	6,901	3,185	2,760
275	Silverware and plated ware....................	11,361	2.0 cir	1,214		4,994		2,998	
276	Smelting and refining copper..................	14,514	2.0 cir	1,443		49,287		4,827	
277	Smelting and refining lead....................	4,036	0	1,374		62,834		4,838	
278	Smelting and refining zinc....................	11,265	?	1,488		10,267		3,569	
279	Tin foil, etc..................................	1,669	?	1,410		10,641		3,956	
280	Watch cases..................................	2,451	?	1,288		4,226		2,520	
	TOTAL......................................	270,327	....	1,292		10,300		3,175	
	MACHINERY, NOT INCLUDING TRANSPORTATION EQUIPMENT								
281	Agricultural implements, incl. tractors.......	77,512	2.0 cir	1,572		7,286		3,590	
282	Cash registers and calculators, etc............	23,630	.1 cir	1,584		5,843		4,944	
283	Typewriters and parts........................	21,440	0	1,211		2,099		1,474	
284	Cranes, dredging, road building machinery ...	18,800	.5 cir	1,497		7,386		3,971	
285	Electrical machinery and supplies............	257,660	0.5	1,382	1,088	6,295	7,890	3,800	3,670
286	Engines, turbines, water wheels, windmills....	32,855	.3	1,547		5,926		3,290	
287	Machinery not elsewhere classified............	146,712	4.1	1,484	1,074	6,572	5,253	4,011	3,051
288	Machine shop products........................	109,245	3.3	1,422	1,145	5,975	4,610	3,576	3,015
289	Machine tool accessories and precision tools...	32,893	.1 cir	1,701		4,928		3,526	
290	Machine tools................................	47,266	.6 cir	1,656		5,506		3,853	
291	Printers' machinery and equipment...........	13,716	1.0 cir	1,632		5,733		4,204	
292	Pumps and pumping equipment...............	28,320	.5 cir	1,404		7,017		4,013	
293	Radios, radio tubes and phonographs.........	48,343	?	1,076		5,746		2,542	
294	Refrigerators and ice-making machinery......	50,623	2.0 cir	1,410		7,186		3,330	
295	Scales and balances...........................	3,299	6.0 cir	1,247		5,413		3,637	
296	Sewing machines..............................	9,019	0	1,502		3,862		2,864	
297	Textile machinery and parts...................	25,340	4.5	1,308	967	4,239	3,830	2,837	2,279
298	Washing machines, household.................	9,302	0	1,255		7,513		3,083	
	TOTAL......................................	955,975	....	1,441		6,160		3,622	

Percentages of wage earners in the Southeast in italics and marked *cir* are estimated. For method see p. 81.

THE STATISTICAL PICTURE

United States and the Southeast *(Continued)*

Percent wages are of value added by manufacture		Salary per salaried person		Salary per wage earner		Wage earners per salaried person		Wage and salary per wage earner		Percent wages and salary are of value added by manufacture		Balance per wage earner for interest, profits, taxes, etc.		
39.9		$ 2,082		$ 462		4.5		$ 1,875		52.8		$ 1,677		238
46.8		2,668		224		11.9		1,520		54.8		1,255		239
56.1		2,111		189		11.2		1,601		63.6		914		240
46.4		3,100		336		9.2		1,851		56.7		1,414		241
62.1	51.3	2,501	2,076	189	234	13.3	8.8	1,510	1,198	70.9	63.8	619	679	242
39.8		4,304		658		6.5		1,888		60.9		1,210		243
49.4		2,083		321		6.5		1,553		62.2		944		244
43.1	55.5	2,127	2,249	340	153	6.3	14.7	1,592	1,018	54.8	65.3	1,311	540	245
43.6		2,376		378		6.3		1,507		58.2		1,081		246
48.0		2,234		260		8.5		1,474		58.3		1,054		247
46.8		2,226		446		5.0		1,723		61.9		1,061		248
44.9		2,577		334		7.7		1,606		56.6		1,231		249
46.7		2,776		353		7.9		1,670		59.2		1,149		250
52.4		2,642		345		7.7		1,832		64.5		1,008		251
50.1		2,494		320		7.8		1,517		63.5		871		252
41.2		2,198		289		7.6		1,470		51.2		1,399		253
52.0		2,694		228		11.8		1,855		59.4		1,268		254
43.7	41.6	2,342	2,303	522	534	4.5	4.3	1,911	1,639	60.3	61.8	1,260	1,013	255
32.7		2,166		339		6.4		1,461		42.6		1,969		256
43.0		2,344		395		5.9		1,595		57.2		1,192		257
41.5		2,530		326		7.8		1,708		51.3		1,619		258
45.5		2,577		339		7.6		1,510		58.6		1,066		259
43.0		2,849		230		12.4		1,606		50.2		1,590		260
48.5		2,468		278		8.9		1,706		58.0		1,234		
45.9		2,203		321		6.9		1,667		56.8		1,268		261
46.1		2,222		245		9.1		1,432		55.9		1,130		262
47.8		3,120		285		11.0		1,229		62.3		744		263
49.4		2,302		299		7.7		1,489		61.9		918		264
26.4		1,772		723		2.4		2,069		40.6		3,029		265
48.2		2,371		379		6.2		1,203		70.4		506		266
22.7		2,761		1,097		2.5		2,535		39.9		3,811		267
44.2		2,127		407		5.2		1,550		59.9		1,037		268
42.7		2,716		527		5.2		1,757		61.0		1,123		269
41.8		2,326		413		5.6		1,559		57.0		1,178		270
39.2		2,152		366		5.9		1,426		52.6		1,283		271
41.8		2,362		335		7.0		1,726		51.8		1,607		272
31.5		2,666		587		4.5		1,788		46.9		2,024		273
40.0	34.3	2,342	1,983	472	392	5.0	5.1	1,746	1,340	54.8	48.6	1,439	1,420	274
40.5		1,964		326		6.0		1,540		51.4		1,458		275
29.9		2,159		284		7.6		1,727		35.8		3,100		276
28.4		2,276		379		6.0		1,753		36.2		3,085		277
41.6		2,728		263		10.4		1,751		49.1		1,818		278
35.7		2,083		308		6.8		1,718		43.4		2,238		279
51.0		2,327		396		5.9		1,684		66.8		836		280
40.6		2,291		354		6.5		1,646		51.8		1,529		
43.8		1,992		314		6.3		1,886		52.5		1,704		281
32.0		2,147		442		4.9		2,026		41.0		2,918		282
82.0		1,672		116		14.4		1,327		90.0		147		283
37.7		2,277		493		4.6		1,990		50.1		1,981		284
36.3	29.7	2,227	2,017	519	474	4.3	4.2	1,901	1,562	50.0	42.6	1,899	2,108	285
47.0		2,183		541		4.0		2,088		63.5		1,202		286
37.0	35.2	2,374	2,158	590	430	4.0	5.0	2,074	1,504	51.7	49.3	1,937	1,547	287
39.8	38.0	2,441	2,127	466	376	5.2	5.6	1,888	1,521	52.8	50.4	1,688	1,494	288
48.3		2,960		468		6.3		2,169		61.5		1,357		289
43.0		2,439		542		4.5		2,198		57.0		1,655		290
38.8		2,151		545		3.9		2,177		51.8		2,027		291
35.2		2,100		569		3.7		1,973		49.2		2,040		292
42.1		2,162		368		5.9		1,444		56.8		1,098		293
42.4		2,234		290		7.7		1,700		51.0		1,630		294
34.3		2,002		510		3.9		1,757		48.3		1,880		295
52.5		2,289		298		7.7		1,800		62.8		1,064		296
46.1	42.5	2,467	2,414	372	295	6.6	8.2	1,680	1,262	59.2	55.4	1,157	1,017	297
40.7		2,022		277		7.3		1,532		49.7		1,551		298
39.8		2,282		468		4.8		1,909		52.7		1,713		

Figures in bold-faced type are indices for the portion of the industry that is located in the Southeast.

INDICES OF MANUFACTURING INDUSTRIES, 1937—

	Industries	Total wage earners	Percent wage earners in S.E.	Wages per wage earner		Value of product per wage earner		Value added by manufacture per wage earner	
	TRANSPORTATION EQUIPMENT, AIR, LAND, AND WATER								
299	Aircraft and parts	24,003	0	$ 1,390		$ 4,440		$ 2,823	
300	Carriages, wagons, sleighs, and sleds	1,823	2.0 cir	945		5,013		2,471	
301	Cars, electric and steam	40,466	4.0 cir	1,465		8,287		2,689	
302	Locomotives, railroad, mining and industrial	9,000	?	1,649		8,014		3,651	
303	Motorcycles, bicycles, and parts	6,938	?	1,183		5,195		2,342	
304	Motor vehicles	194,527	2.0 cir	1,625		15,917		3,608	
305	Motor-vehicle bodies and parts	284,814	1.0 cir	1,545		7,303		2,826	
306	Ship and boat building	62,274	18.0 cir	1,505		4,022		2,393	
	TOTAL	623,845		1,552		9,620		3,035	
	MISCELLANEOUS INDUSTRIES								
307	Artists' materials	372	0	1,082		7,460		4,036	
308	Beauty shop equipment	2,548	2.0 cir	973		5,326		3,233	
309	Brooms	4,067	18.4	714	525	2,859	2,114	1,310	994
310	Brushes other than rubber	7,915	1.0 cir	916		5,627		2,581	
311	Buttons	12,026	4.0 cir	770		2,602		1,473	
312	Carbon paper and inked ribbons	1,627	0	1,224		10,977		5,336	
313	Dentists' equipment and supplies	4,574	.5 cir	1,169		6,751		3,971	
314	Fur goods, regular factories	12,798	.1 cir	1,670		12,109		3,810	
315	Fur goods, contract factories	154	0	1,240		4,115		3,216	
316	Furs, dressed and dyed	6,343	.5 cir	1,314		3,431		2,414	
317	Instruments and apparatus, scientific, etc.	17,399	.5 cir	1,353		5,518		3,812	
318	Lapidary work	217	0	1,411		20,233		4,827	
319	Mattresses and bedsprings	19,165	14.6	1,034	782	5,902	4,884	2,605	2,112
320	Musical instruments—pianos	5,698	0	1,239		3,809		2,095	
321	Musical instruments—organs	1,086	0	1,137		4,270		2,912	
322	Musical instruments—piano & organ materials	1,778	0	965		2,800		1,611	
323	Musical instruments and parts, not elsw. clsfd.	3,409	0	1,195		3,505		2,388	
324	Optical goods	11,998	1.0 cir	1,206		3,956		2,753	
325	Pencils and crayons	5,776	8.0 cir	903		3,883		2,175	
326	Pens, pen points	4,343	?	1,002		5,026		3,326	
327	Photograph materials	18,450	.5 cir	1,565		6,281		4,294	
328	Pipes (tobacco)	2,382	0	1,013		3,210		2,151	
329	Roofing, asphalt shingles, etc.	7,418	3.0 cir	1,283		13,826		5,381	
330	Signs and advertising novelties	16,042	5.0 cir	1,196		4,720		2,990	
331	Sporting and athletic goods	11,392	5.0 cir	1,030		3,903		1,984	
332	Steam and other packings	5,934	2.0 cir	1,168		5,486		2,950	
333	Surgical and orthopedic appliances	8,423	1.0 cir	1,015		9,150		3,804	
334	Cigarettes	26,149	94.7	925	922	17,500*	17,358*	7,549	7,696
335	Cigars	55,879	22.0 cir	671		2,799*		1,466	
336	Tobacco—chewing, smoking, and snuff	10,130	48.0 cir	848		9,590		4,517	
337	Toys	17,547	2.0 cir	856		3,639		1,997	
338	Toys, children's carriages and sleds	5,218	0	1,038		3,767		1,858	
339	Umbrellas and canes	3,088	1.0 cir	833		4,287		1,683	
340	Window shades and fixtures	3,166	3.0 cir	1,002		7,446		3,247	
341	Artificial and preserved flowers	5,657	†	688		2,542		1,461	
342	Feathers and plumes	559	†	782		4,150		2,015	
343	Foundry supplies	466	†	1,270		18,510		8,340	
344	Hair work	434	†	861		5,643		3,472	
345	Hand stamps and stencils	2,375	†	1,233		4,373		3,090	
346	Jewelry and instrument cases	4,788	†	771		2,549		1,534	
347	Miscellaneous articles not elsewhere classified	15,854	†	814		3,432		1,908	
348	Models and patterns (not paper)	5,728	†	1,704		3,891		3,168	
349	Paving materials—blocks and mixtures	1,946	†	1,243		12,995		5,490	
350	Soda fountains and related products	1,655	†	1,541		7,860		4,085	
351	Theatrical scenery and stage equipment	397	†	1,232		6,720		3,750	
352	Wool pulling	794	†	1,340		20,970		4,978	
	TOTAL	355,164		1,033		7,650		3,040	
	UNITED STATES—ALL INDUSTRIES	8,569,231		1,180		7,085		2,938	

*Internal revenue tax deducted. †No data by states.
Percentages of wage earners in the Southeast in italics and marked *cir* are estimated. For method see p. 81.

THE STATISTICAL PICTURE

UNITED STATES AND THE SOUTHEAST (Continued)

Percent wages are of value added by manufacture		Salary per salaried person		Salary per wage earner		Wage earners per salaried person		Wage and salary per wage earner		Percent wages and salary are of value added by manufacture		Balance per wage earner for interest, profits, taxes, etc.		
49.2		$ 1,751		$ 563		3.1		$ 1,953		69.2		$ 870		299
38.3		2,002		328		6.1		1,273		51.5		1,198		300
54.5		2,014		224		9.0		1,689		62.8		1,000		301
45.2		2,258		499		4.5		2,148		58.8		1,503		302
50.5		2,128		269		7.9		1,452		62.0		890		303
45.1		2,166		250		8.6		1,875		52.0		1,733		304
54.7		2,312		230		10.0		1,775		62.8		1,051		305
63.0		2,526		309		8.2		1,814		75.8		579		306
51.2		2,208		262		8.4		1,814		59.8		1,221		
26.8		2,248		870		2.6		1,952		48.4		2,084		307
30.1		2,412		560		4.3		1,533		47.4		1,700		308
54.5	52.9	1,580	1,265	148	108	10.6	11.7	862	633	65.8	63.7	448	361	309
35.4		2,277		339		6.7		1,255		48.6		1,326		310
52.4		2,197		193		11.4		963		65.4		510		311
22.9		2,784		842		3.3		2,066		38.7		3,270		312
29.4		2,476		570		4.3		1,739		43.8		2,232		313
43.8		2,405		579		4.2		2,249		59.0		1,561		314
38.6		1,726		247		7.0		1,487		46.2		1,729		315
54.4		3,494		316		4.0		1,630		67.5		784		316
35.5		2,262		674		3.4		2,027		53.2		1,785		317
29.2		2,213		551		4.0		1,962		40.6		2,865		318
39.7	37.0	2,094	2,451	346	344	6.0	7.1	1,380	1,126	53.0	53.3	1,225	986	319
59.0		1,997		197		10.2		1,436		68.5		659		320
39.0		2,619		551		5.6		1,688		58.0		1,224		321
59.8		2,991		262		11.4		1,227		76.2		384		322
50.0		2,053		414		5.0		1,609		67.4		779		323
43.7		2,210		455		4.8		1,661		60.3		1,092		324
41.5		2,480		314		7.9		1,217		56.0		958		325
30.1		1,876		355		5.3		1,357		40.8		1,969		326
36.4		2,274		587		3.9		2,152		50.1		2,142		327
47.2		2,290		170		13.4		1,183		55.0		968		328
23.8		2,097		312		6.7		1,595		29.6		3,786		329
40.1		2,131		507		4.2		1,703		57.0		1,287		330
52.0		1,943		278		7.0		1,308		65.9		676		331
39.5		2,362		439		5.4		1,607		54.5		1,343		332
26.6		1,928		434		4.4		1,449		38.1		2,355		333
12.2	12.0	2,459	2,455	142	138	17.4	17.7	1,067	1,060	14.1	13.8	6,482	6,636	334
45.8		1,873		102		18.4		773		52.7		693		335
18.8		2,339		267		8.8		1,115		24.7		3,402		336
42.9		2,173		254		8.6		1,110		55.6		887		337
55.8		2,187		215		10.2		1,253		67.4		605		338
49.5		2,318		209		11.1		1,042		61.9		641		339
30.8		1,989		432		4.6		1,434		44.2		1,813		340
47.1		2,056		175		11.8		863		59.1		598		341
39.0		2,320		332		7.0		1,114		55.3		901		342
15.2		2,788		1,250		2.2		1,520		18.2		6,820		343
24.9		2,863		600		4.8		1,461		42.1		2,011		344
40.0		2,051		785		2.6		2,018		65.3		1,072		345
50.3		2,513		246		10.2		1,017		66.3		517		346
42.6		2,034		290		7.0		1,104		57.9		804		347
53.8		2,752		436		6.3		2,140		67.6		1,028		348
22.7		1,938		508		3.8		1,751		31.9		3,739		349
37.6		2,205		514		4.3		2,055		50.3		2,030		350
32.9		2,333		752		3.1		1,984		52.9		1,766		351
27.0		3,340		341		9.8		1,681		33.8		3,297		352
34.0		2,212		329		6.7		1,362		44.8		1,678		
40.2		2,232		317		7.0		1,497		51.0		1,441		

Figures in bold-faced type are indices for the portion of the industry that is located in the Southeast.

INDEX

(Double page numbers following each industry refer to indices in tables, Chapter V)

A

Abrasives, 90-91
Agricultural implements, including tractors, 92-93
Agricultural products. See Resources; Markets
Aircraft and parts, 94-95
Alabama, indices, 9
Aluminum products, 92-93; potential industry for Southeast, 63
Ammunition and related products, 88-89
Arizona, indices, 9
Arkansas, indices, 9
Art goods. See Statuary
Artificial and preserved flowers, 94-95
Artificial leather, 86-87; potential industry for Southeast, 61
Artists' materials, 94-95
Asbestos products other than steam packings, 90-91
Asphalt-felt-base floor covering, 86-87; potential industry for Southeast, 61
Awnings, tents, sails, canvas covers, 86-87; potential industry for Southeast, 41

B

Bags. See Trunks
Bags, other than paper, 86-87; quota industry in Southeast, 27
Bags, paper, not made in paper mills, 88-89; quota industry in Southeast, 23-24
Bakery products. See Bread
Baking powder, yeast, etc., 88-89
Balanced production, industries for, 55, 65; need for in Southeast, 79
Banners. See Flags, etc.
Barrels. See Steel barrels; Cooperage
Baskets and willow ware, 88-89; quota industry in Southeast, 22
Batting and padding, 86-87; potential industry for Southeast, 42
Beauty shop equipment, 94-95
Bedspreads. See Curtains, etc.
Bedsprings. See Mattresses and bedsprings

Beet sugar. See Sugar
Beverages, nonalcoholic, 84-85; quota industry in Southeast, 28-29
Bicycles. See Motorcycles
Billiard and pool tables, bowling alleys, 88-89
Blacking, stains, and dressings, 88-89
Blank books. See Bookbinding
Blast-furnace products, 90-91
Blouses, contract factories, 86-87
Blouses, regular factories, 86-87
Bluing, 88-89
Boiler shop products, 90-91
Bolts, nuts, not made in rolling mills, 90-91; potential industry for Southeast, 63
Bone black, carbon black, 88-89; potential industry for Southeast, 44
Book, music and job printing, 88-89; potential industry for Southeast, 43
Bookbinding and blank-book making, 88-89; potential industry for Southeast, 44
Boot and shoe cut stock, 90-91
Boots and shoes, other than rubber, 90-91; potential industry for Southeast, 59-60
Bowling alleys. See Billiard tables
Boxes, cigar, 88-89; quota industry in Southeast, 22
Boxes, paper, 88-89; potential industry for Southeast, 43
Boxes, wooden, except cigar, 88-89; quota industry in Southeast, 21-22
Bread and other bakery products, 84-85; potential industry for Southeast, 36-37
Bricks. See Clay products
Brooms, 94-95; potential industry for Southeast, 50-51
Brushes other than rubber, 94-95
Butter, 84-85; potential industry for Southeast, 56-57
Buttons, 94-95

C

California, indices, 9
Candles, 88-89
Cane sugar. See Sugar

[97]

INDEX

Canned and cured fish, etc., 84-85; quota industry in Southeast, 29
Canned and dried fruits, vegetables, etc., 84-85; potential industry for Southeast, 38-39
Canvas covers. See Awnings, etc.
Capital investment, lack of statistics on, 6, 8; estimated in cigarettes, 12; cane sugar manufacture, 13; cotton yarn, 16; cotton goods, 16; cottonseed oil, 18; fertilizers, 19; cast iron pipe, 20; furniture, 23; pulp, 23; rayon, 24; cotton cutting-up industries, 27; cane sugar refining, 28; beverages, nonalcoholic, 28; bread, etc., 37; confectionery, 40; chemicals, 45; paints, etc., 45; drugs and medicines, 46; cement, 48; iron and steel, 49, 63; flour milling, 55; malt liquors, 56; dairy products, 57; meat packing, 58; soap, 60; linoleum, etc., 61
Caps, men's and boys'. See Hats
Carbon black. See Bone black, etc.
Carbon paper and inked ribbons, 94-95
Card cutting and designing, 88-89
Cardboard, not made in paper mills, 88-89
Carpet yarn, 84-85; potential industry for Southeast, 59
Carpets and rugs, paper, fiber, and grass, 84-85
Carpets and rugs, rag, 84-85
Carpets and rugs, wool, 84-85; potential industry for Southeast, 59
Carriages, wagons, sleighs, and sleds, 94-95
Cars, electric and steam, 94-95
Cash registers and calculators, etc., 92-93
Caskets, coffins, etc., 88-89; potential industry for Southeast, 42
Cast iron pipe and fittings, 90-91; majority industry in Southeast, 20
Cement, 90-91; potential industry for Southeast, 48
Cereal preparations, 84-85
Cheese, 84-85; potential industry for Southeast, 57
Chemicals not elsewhere classified, 88-89; potential industry for Southeast, 44-45
Chewing gum, 84-85
Children's clothing. See Outerwear; Underwear
China firing not done in potteries, 90-91
Chocolate and cocoa products, 84-85
Cigarettes, 94-95; monopoly industry in Southeast, 11-13
Cigar boxes. See Boxes
Cigars, 94-95; quota industry in Southeast, 30
Clay products other than pottery; 90-91; potential industry for Southeast, 47-48
Cleaning and polishing preparations, 88-89
Clocks, watches, time recording devices, 92-93
Clothing. See Men's and boys' etc.; Blouses; Coats and suits; Dresses, etc.; Underwear, etc.
Clothing, women's and misses', not elsewhere classified, contract factories, 86-87
Clothing, women's and misses', not elsewhere classified, regular factories, 86-87
Coats, suits, etc., women's and misses', contract factories, 86-87
Coats, suits, etc., women's and misses', regular factories, 86-87
Coffins. See Caskets
Coke oven products, 90-91; potential industry for Southeast, 47
Collapsible tubes, 92-93
Collars. See Shirts
Colorado, indices, 9
Compressed and liquefied gases, 88-89; potential industry for Southeast, 46-47
Concrete products, 90-91; potential industry for Southeast, 48
Condensed and evaporated milk, 84-85; potential industry for Southeast, 57
Confectionery, 84-85; potential industry for Southeast, 40
Connecticut, indices, 9
Cooking apparatus. See Heating, etc.
Cooperage, 88-89; quota industry in Southeast, 22
Copper. See Smelting, etc.
Cordage and twine, 84-85; quota industry in Southeast, 26
Cork products, 88-89
Corn sirup, etc. and starch, 84-85; potential industry for Southeast, 56
Corsets and allied garments, 86-87
Cotton cutting-up industries, 26-28. See also specific garment industries
Cotton goods woven (over 12 inches), 84-85; majority industry in Southeast, 16-17
Cotton narrow fabrics, 84-85
Cotton yarn and thread, 84-85; majority industry in Southeast, 15-16
Cottonseed oil, cake and meal, 90-91; majority industry in Southeast, 18-19
Cranes and dredging, road building machinery, 92-93
Crops. See Resources
Curtains, draperies, and bedspreads, contract factories, 86-87
Curtains, draperies, and bedspreads, regular factories, 86-87; quota industry in Southeast, 27
Cutlery (not silver and plated) and edge tools, 90-91
Cutting-up industries. See Cotton

D

Defense program, effect on iron and steel industries in Southeast, 50; and opportunity for diversification, 78-80
Delaware, indices, 9
Dentists' equipment and supplies, 94-95

INDEX

Distilled liquors. See Liquors
District of Columbia, indices, 9
Diversification, need of markets, 54-55; of industry in Southeast, 70-71
Doors, shutters, sash frames, etc., 92-93
Draperies. See Curtains, etc.
Dresses, except house, contract factories, 86-87
Dresses, except house, regular factories, 86-87
Dresses, house, uniforms, etc., contract factories, 86-87
Dresses, house, uniforms, etc., regular factories, 86-87
Drug grinding, 88-89
Drugs and medicines, 88-89; potential industry for Southeast, 46
Dyeing and finishing cotton fabrics, 84-85; quota industry in Southeast, 26
Dyeing and finishing rayon and silk, 84-85
Dyeing and finishing yarn, 84-85

E

Edge tools. See Cutlery
Electrical machinery and supplies, 92-93
Electroplating, 92-93
Electrotyping. See Stereotyping
Embroideries—other than Schiffli, contract factories, 86-87
Embroideries—other than Schiffli, regular factories, 86-87
Embroideries—Schiffli machine, contract factories, 86-87
Embroideries—Schiffli machine, regular factories, 86-87
Engines, turbines, water wheels, windmills, 92-93
Engraving, chasing, etching, etc., 88-89
Engraving, steel, copper, wood, 88-89
Envelopes, 88-89
Evaporated milk. See Condensed and evaporated milk
Excelsior, 88-89; quota industry in Southeast, 22
Explosives, 88-89

F

Fabricated textile products not elsewhere classified, 86-87
Far West, indices, 9
Feathers and plumes, 94-95
Feeds, prepared, for animals, 84-85; potential industry for Southeast, 38
Felt goods (except woven felts), 84-85
Fertilizers, 88-89; majority industry in Southeast, 19
Files, 92-93
Fire extinguishers, chemical, 92-93
Firearms, 92-93
Fireworks, 88-89
Fish nets and seines, 84-85

Flags, banners, vestments, and robes, 86-87
Flavoring extracts and sirups, 84-85
Florida, indices, 9
Flour and other grain mill products, 84-85; potential industry for Southeast, 55-56
Foods not elsewhere classified, 84-85; potential industry for Southeast, 39, 59
Forgings, not made in rolling mills, 92-93; potential industry for Southeast, 63
Foundry products, 92-93; potential industry for Southeast, 49-50
Foundry supplies, 94-95
Fuel briquets, 90-91
Fur goods, contract factories, 94-95
Fur goods, regular factories, 94-95
Furnishings. See House, etc.; Men's furnishing goods
Furniture (household), 88-89; quota industry in Southeast, 22-23
Furniture, office, etc., 88-89
Furs, dressed and dyed, 94-95

G

Galvanizing and other coating, 92-93
Garters. See Suspenders
Gases. See Compressed and liquefied gases
Gelatin. See Glue
Georgia, indices, 9
Glass, 90-91; potential industry for Southeast, 48-49
Gloves and mittens, cloth or cloth and leather, 86-87
Gloves and mittens, leather, 90-91
Glue and gelatin, 88-89; potential industry for Southeast, 63
Gold leaf and foil, 92-93
Gold, silver and platinum-refining and alloying, 92-93
Grain milling. See Flour and other grain mill products
Granite. See Marble, etc.
Graphite, ground and refined, 90-91
Grease and tallow, 88-89; potential industry for Southeast, 59-60
Gypsum products, 90-91

H

Hair work, 94-95
Handbags and purses, women's, 90-91
Handkerchiefs, contract factories, 86-87
Handkerchiefs, regular factories, 86-87
Hand stamps and stencils, 94-95
Hardware not elsewhere classified, 92-93
Harness. See Saddlery
Hat bodies—carded wool felt, 84-85
Hat and cap materials, men's, 84-85
Hats and caps, except felt and straw, men's, 84-85
Hats, fur-felt, 84-85
Hats, straw, men's, 84-85

INDEX

Heath, Milton S., Study of Southern Industry by, 79
Heating and cooking apparatus, except electric, 92-93; potential industry for Southeast, 49-50
High value of product, industries with, 64, 66 (chart), 68-69
Highest value-added industries, list of, 33
Highest wage industries, list of, 32
Hosiery, 84-85; quota industry in Southeast, 25-26
House furnishings not elsewhere classified, 86-87
Household furniture. See Furniture

I

Ice. See Manufactured ice
Ice cream, 84-85; potential industry for Southeast, 37-38
Idaho, indices, 9
Illinois, indices, 9
Indiana, indices, 9
Indices. See Wage earner index; specific industries
Industry, methods for securing, 3; need for in South, 3; diversity of in South, 70-71
Ink, printing, 88-89
Ink, writing, 88-89
Insecticides, etc., 88-89; potential industry for Southeast, 47
Instruments and apparatus, scientific, etc., 94-95
Insulation board. See Wallboard
Iowa, indices, 9

J

Jewelers' findings and materials, 92-93
Jewelry, 92-93
Jewelry and instrument cases, 94-95
Jute goods, 84-85

K

Kansas, indices, 9
Kentucky, indices, 9
Knitted cloth, 84-85
Knitted gloves and mittens, 84-85
Knitted outerwear, contract factories, 84-85
Knitted outerwear, regular factories, 84-85
Knitted underwear, 84-85; quota industry in Southeast, 26

L

Labor, abundance of, 70. See also Skills
Lace goods, 84-85
Lapidary work, 94-95
Lasts and related products, 88-89
Lead. See Smelting, etc.
Leather, belting and packing, 90-91
Leather goods, not elsewhere classified, 90-91
Leather goods, small articles, 90-91
Leather, tanned, etc., contract factories, 90-91
Leather, tanned, etc., regular factories, 90-91; potential industry for Southeast, 59-60
Lighting equipment, 92-93
Lime, 90-91; quota industry in Southeast, 29
Linen goods, 84-85
Linoleum, 86-87; potential industry for Southeast, 61
Linseed oil and cake, 90-91; potential industry for Southeast, 60-61
Liquefied gases. See Compressed and liquefied gases
Liquors, distilled, 84-85; quota industry in Southeast, 29
Liquors, malt, 84-85; potential industry for Southeast, 56
Liquors, rectified and blended, 84-85
Liquors, vinous, 84-85
Lithographing, 88-89; potential industry for Southeast, 62
Locomotives, railroad, mining, and industrial, 94-95
Louisiana, indices, 9
Low value of product, industries with, 64, 67 (chart), 68-69
Lowest value-added industries, list of, 31
Lowest wage industries, list of, 30
Lubricating oils (not made in petroleum refineries), 90-91
Lumber and timber products, 88-89; quota industries in Southeast, 21

M

Macaroni, 84-85
Machine shop products, 92-93
Machine tool accessories and precision tools, 92-93
Machine tools, 92-93
Machinery not elsewhere classified, 92-93
Maine, indices, 9
Malt, 84-85; potential industry for Southeast, 56
Malt liquors. See Liquors
Manufactured ice, 84-85; quota industry in Southeast, 29
Marble, granite, etc., cut and shaped, 90-91; quota industry in Southeast, 29
Markets, need for in Southeast, 54-55, 70; industries furnishing, 65
Maryland, indices, 9
Massachusetts, indices, 9
Matches, 88-89
Mattresses and bedsprings, 94-95; potential industry for Southeast, 51
Meat packing, 84-85; potential industry for Southeast, 58
Medicines. See Drugs
Men's and boys' clothing, leather and sheep lined, 86-87
Men's and boys' clothing, not elsewhere classified, contract factories, 86-87

INDEX

Men's and boys' clothing, not elsewhere classified, regular factories, 86-87
Men's and boys' trousers, wash suits, etc., apparel, 86-87; quota industry in Southeast, 27
Men's and boys' underwear, contract factories, 86-87
Men's and boys' underwear, regular factories, 86-87
Men's and boys' work and sport clothing, not leather, 86-87; quota industry in Southeast, 27
Men's furnishing goods, not elsewhere classified, contract factories, 86-87
Men's furnishing goods, not elsewhere classified, regular factories, 86-87
Michigan, indices, 9
Middle States, indices, 9
Milk. See Condensed and evaporated milk
Millinery, contract factories, 86-87
Millinery, regular factories, 86-87
Minerals and earths, ground, etc., 90-91
Minnesota, indices, 9
Mirror and picture frames, 88-89
Mirrors, etc., 90-91
Miscellaneous articles not elsewhere classified, 94-95
Miscellaneous food preparations. See Food not elsewhere classified
Miscellaneous hand tools, 92-93
Mississippi, indices, 9
Missouri, indices, 9
Mittens. See Knitted gloves and mittens; Gloves
Models and patterns (not paper), 94-95
Montana, indices, 9
Motorcycles, bicycles, and parts, 94-95
Motor-vehicle bodies and parts, 94-95
Motor vehicles, 94-95
Mucilage, etc., 88-89
Music printing. See Book printing
Musical instruments and parts, not elsewhere classified, 94-95
Musical instruments—organs, 94-95
Musical instruments—pianos, 94-95
Musical instruments—piano and organ materials, 94-95

N

Nails, spikes, etc., not made in rolling mills, 92-93
National defense. See Defense program
Natural resources. See Resources
Nebraska, indices, 9
Needles, pins, hooks and eyes, fasteners, 92-93
Negro, in cigarette industry, 11; in cane sugar manufacture, 13; in fertilizers, 19
Nevada, indices, 9
New Hampshire, indices, 9
New Jersey, indices, 9

New Mexico, indices, 9
New York, indices, 9
Newspaper and periodical printing, 88-89
Nightwear. See Shirts, etc.
North Carolina, indices, 9
North Dakota, indices, 9
Northeast, indices, 9
Northwest, indices, 9
Nonclay refractories, 90-91
Nonferrous alloys and products, except aluminum, 92-93
Nonferrous metals. See Smelting, etc.
Nuts. See Bolts

O

Odum, Howard W., footnote 5
Office furniture. See Furniture
Ohio, indices, 9
Oilcloth, 86-87
Oils, essential, 90-91
Oils not elsewhere classified, 90-91; potential industry for Southeast, 47
Oils, salad. See Shortenings
Oklahoma, indices, 9
Oleomargarine, 84-85; potential industry for Southeast, 63
Opportunity, for southern youth, 77-78; of national defense program, 78-80
Optical goods, 94-95
Optimum production, definition, 5-6; in Southeast in Group I industries, 11; and opportunity, 77-78
Oregon, indices, 9
Organs. See Musical instruments
Outerwear, children's, regular factories, 86-87

P

Padding. See Batting and padding
Paints, pigments and varnish, 90-91; potential industry for Southeast, 45-46
Paper, 88-89; potential industry for Southeast, 43
Paper goods not elsewhere classified, 88-89. See also Bags; Boxes
Paving materials—blocks and mixtures, 94-95
Pencils and crayons, 94-95
Pennsylvania, indices, 9
Pens, pen points, 94-95
Perfumes, cosmetics, etc., 90-91
Periodicals. See Newspaper printing
Petroleum refining, 90-91
Phonographs. See Radios, etc.
Photoengraving, not in printing establishments, 88-89; potential industry for Southeast, 62
Photographic materials, 94-95
Pianos. See Musical instruments
Picture frames. See Mirrors
Pins. See Needles, etc.
Pipe. See Cast iron pipe

INDEX

Pipes (tobacco), 94-95
Planing mill products, 88-89; quota industry in Southeast, 22
Planning, interest in, 4-5; need for, 4; field for, 54
Plumbers' supplies (not pipe or vitreous china), 92-93
Polishing preparations. See Cleaning preparations
Pool tables. See Billiard tables
Population, basis for regional proportion of manufacturing, 10
Porcelain. See Pottery
Pottery and porcelain, 90-91; potential industry for Southeast, 62
Poultry dressing and packing, 84-85; potential industry for Southeast, 58
Printers' machinery and equipment, 92-93
Processed waste, 86-87
Pulp (wood and other fiber), 88-89; quota industry in Southeast, 23
Pumps and pumping equipment, 92-93
Purses. See Handbags

R

Radios, radio tubes and phonographs, 92-93
Rayon and allied products, 90-91; quota industry in Southeast, 24
Rayon narrow fabrics, 84-85
Rayon throwing and spinning, 84-85
Rayon woven goods, 84-85; quota industry in Southeast, 24-25
Rayon yarn and thread (processed for sale), 86-87
Refining. See Petroleum; Sugar
Refrigerators and ice-making machinery, 92-93
Regional percentages of industries, methods of calculating, 81
Resources, basis for chief industries in Southeast, 10, 36, 70
Rhode Island, indices, 9
Rice cleaning and polishing, 84-85; majority industry in Southeast, 17
Road building machinery. See Cranes, etc.
Robes. See Flags, etc.
Rolling mill products. See Steel-works and rolling mill products
Roofing, asphalt shingles, etc., 94-95
Rubber boots and shoes, 90-91
Rubber goods (other than above), 90-91
Rubber tires and tubes, 90-91
Rugs. See Carpets

S

Saddlery, harness, and whips, 90-91
Safes and vaults, 92-93
Sails. See Awning, etc.
Salad oils. See Shortenings
Salt, 90-91
Sand-lime brick, 90-91
Sausage casings, 84-85
Sausages, meat puddings, etc., 84-85; potential industry for Southeast, 58-59
Saws, 92-93
Scales and balances, 92-93
Screens. See Windows and door screens
Screw-machine products and wood screws, 92-93
Sewing machines, 92-93
Sheet-metal work not specifically classified, 92-93
Ship and boat building, 94-95; potential industry for Southeast, 50
Shirts (except work), collars, nightwear, contract factories, 86-87
Shirts (except work), collars, nightwear, regular factories, 86-87; in southeastern states, 27, 41
Shoes. See Boots and shoes
Shortenings, cooking and salad oils, 84-85; potential industry for Southeast, 40
Signs and advertising novelties, 94-95
Silk broad woven goods, 86-87
Silk narrow fabrics, 86-87
Silk throwing and spinning (commission only), 86-87
Silk yarn and thread (made for sale), 86-87
Silverware and plated ware, 92-93
Sirups. See Flavoring extracts and sirups
Skills, deficiency in Southeast, 8, 70-73; types of, needed, 74-76; development of, in Southeast, 76, 77-78
Smelting and refining copper, 92-93
Smelting and refining lead, 92-93
Smelting and refining nonferrous metals, 92-93
Smelting and refining zinc, 92-93
Soap, 90-91; potential industry for Southeast, 59-60
Soda fountains and related products, 94-95
South Carolina, indices, 9
South Dakota, indices, 9
Southeast, indices, 9; percentages of factors in manufacturing, 7; population base for manufacturing, 10
Southern Regions of the United States, 5
Southwest, indices, 9
Sporting and athletic goods, 94-95
Springs, steel, except wire, not made in rolling mills, 92-93
Stamped and pressed metal products, 92-93
Starch. See Corn sirup and starch
Statuary and art goods (factory), 90-91
Steam and other packings, 94-95
Steel barrels, kegs, and drums, 92-93
Steel-works and rolling mill products, 92-93
Stereotyping and electrotyping, not in printing establishments, 88-89
Structural and ornamental steel, not in rolling mills, 92-93

INDEX

Sugar, beet, 84-85
Sugar, cane, production, 84-85; monopoly industry in Southeast, 13-14
Sugar, cane, refining, 84-85; quota industry in Southeast, 28
Suitcases. See Trunks, etc.
Suits. See Coats, etc.; Men's and boys' clothing
Surgical and orthopedic appliances, 94-95
Suspenders, garters, etc., 86-87
Synthetic-resin, etc. products, 88-89; potential industry for Southeast, 63

T

Tanning materials, etc., 90-91; quota industry in Southeast, 24
Tennessee, indices, 9
Tents. See Awnings, etc.
Texas, indices, 9
Textile machinery and parts, 92-93
Theatrical scenery and stage equipment, 94-95
Tile. See Clay products
Tin cans and other tinware, 92-93; potential industry for Southeast, 63
Tin foil, etc., 92-93; potential industry for Southeast, 63
Tires. See Rubber tires
Tobacco—chewing, smoking, and snuff, 94-95; quota industry in Southeast, 30-31
Tools. See Machine tools; Miscellaneous hand tools
Toys, 94-95
Toys, children's carriages and sleds, 94-95
Tractors. See Agricultural implements
Trimmings (not made in textile mills), contract factories, 86-87
Trimmings (not made in textile mills), regular factories, 86-87
Trunks, suitcases, and bags, 90-91; potential industry for Southeast, 47
Tubes. See Rubber
Turbines. See Engines
Turpentine and rosin, 88-89; monopoly industry in Southeast, 14
Typewriters and parts, 92-93

U

Umbrellas and canes, 94-95
Underwear, women's and children's knitted, 86-87
Underwear, women's and children's woven, 86-87
United States, indices, 9
Utah, indices, 9

V

Varnish. See Paints and varnish
Vermont, indices, 9
Vestments. See Flags, etc.
Vinegar and cider, 84-85
Vinous liquors. See Liquors

Virginia, indices, 9
Vocational education, need for, 77-78

W

Wage earner index, advantages of, 6; limitations of, 7; comparison of American industries by, 82-84; table of—for all industries, 84-95
Wagons. See Carriages
Wall paper, 88-89
Wallboard, plaster, insulation, 90-91; potential industry for Southeast, 49
Washing machines, household, 92-93
Washington, indices, 9
Waste. See Processed waste
Watch cases, 92-93
Watches. See Clocks, etc.
West Virginia, indices, 9
Whips. See Saddlery
Willow ware. See Baskets
Window and door screens and weather strip, 88-89; potential industry for Southeast, 63
Window shades and fixtures, 94-95
Wine. See Liquors
Wire drawn from purchased rods, 92-93; potential industry for Southeast, 63
Wirework not elsewhere classified, 92-93; potential industry for Southeast, 63
Wisconsin, indices, 9
Women's and misses' clothing. See Blouses; Clothing, etc.; Coats and suits; Dresses; Underwear; Corsets, etc.
Wood distillation, 90-91; majority industry in Southeast, 19-20
Wood preserving, 88-89; quota industry in Southeast, 23
Wood turned and shaped, 88-89; quota industry in Southeast, 22
Wooden boxes. See Boxes
Wool combing, 86-87
Wool pulling, 94-95
Wool scouring, 86-87
Woolen and worsted dyeing and finishing, 86-87
Woolen woven goods and woven felt, 86-87
Woolen yarn, 86-87
Worsted woven goods, 86-87
Worsted yarn, 86-87
Woven felt. See Woolen woven goods; Felt goods
Wrought pipe, not made in rolling mills, 92-93
Wyoming, indices, 9

Y

Yarn. See Carpet yarn; Cotton yarn and thread; Dyeing and finishing yarn; Woolen yarn; Worsted yarn
Youth, opportunities for southern, 77-78

Z

Zinc. See Smelting, etc.

www.ingramcontent.com/pod-product-compliance
Lightning Source LLC
Chambersburg PA
CBHW081834300426
44116CB00014B/2585